Caroline

Isla

Bloomsbury Methuen Drama
An imprint of Bloomsbury Publishing Plc

B L O O M S B U R Y
LONDON • NEW DELHI • NEW YORK • SYDNEY

Bloomsbury Methuen Drama
An imprint of Bloomsbury Publishing Plc

Imprint previously known as Methuen Drama

50 Bedford Square	1385 Broadway
London	New York
WC1B 3DP	NY 10018
UK	USA

www.bloomsbury.com

**BLOOMSBURY, METHUEN DRAMA and the Diana
logo are trademarks of Bloomsbury Publishing Plc**

First published 2015

British Library Cataloguing-in-Publication Data
A catalogue record for this book is available from the British Library.

ISBN: PB: 978-1-4742-4550-0
ePDF: 978-1-4742-4551-7
ePub: 978-1-4742-4552-4

Library in Congress Cataloging in Publication Data
A catalog record for this book is available from the Library of Congress

Series: Modern Plays

Typeset by Mark Heslington Ltd, Scarborough, North Yorkshire
Printed and bound in Great Britain

Island Confidential

John Christensen*

Islands have a special place in our imaginations: as luxurious boltholes from the pressures of modern life, or as lawless hangouts for pirates and smugglers. They offer us an opportunity to fantasise about a different world where we can shake off our responsibilities and take charge of our destinies.

These fantasies of liberation are not always benign. In 1972 Carl Gerstacker, then chief executive of the US company Dow Chemical, manufacturer of the toxic Agent Orange chemicals that US forces had been spraying across Vietnam, declared: 'I have long dreamed of buying an island owned by no nation and of establishing the World Headquarters of the Dow company on the truly neutral ground of such an island, beholden to no nation or society.' He was neither the first, nor the last, person to indulge in these fantasies of escape.

Islanders themselves, however, suffer the yoke of the control mechanisms that regulate small, inward-looking societies. Island life, in the words of author David Guterson, causes 'an inbreeding of the spirit, too much held in, regret and silent brooding, a world whose inhabitants walk in trepidation, in fear of opening up'. Growing up on the British island of Jersey I soon learned that island life can bring out the best and worst in us. On the positive side, islands can breed a truculent independence and encourage self-reliance, à la Robinson Crusoe. Yet islands can also breed social conformism, backwardness, and hostility or indifference towards outsiders. They also instil a strong sense of social hierarchy and deference to wealth and power. On Jersey, I quickly learnt the importance of not 'rocking the boat'. Those few who do resist the consensus – and I became one of them – were confronted with another maritime metaphor: 'There's always the boat in the morning.' If you don't like it, leave.

The control mechanisms and the genuine opportunities of escape that islands can offer help explain why many islands like Jersey have become tax havens. Not all islands are tax havens, and not all tax havens are islands, of course; but islands do tend to provide a particularly hospitable environment for these activities. If local democracy is shackled by island control mechanisms you can draft your laws with minimal domestic interference then sell those laws to the highest bidders – and that means, in today's world, the multinational corporations and wealthy, globe-trotting elites. Robert Kirkby, technical director for Jersey's financial lobbying arm, explained how law-making works: 'Someone comes up with a new idea, but onshore regulation blocks it,' he said in March 2009, in the midst of the global financial crisis. 'You can lobby onshore, but there are lots of stakeholders. In Jersey, you can bash this thing through fast. We can change our company laws and our regulations so much faster than you can in, say, the UK, France or Germany.' This sounds efficient and exciting, until one realises that the stakeholders represent genuine democratic interests. What he was saying is that Jersey will ask no difficult questions of those with money while helping them sidestep democratic controls and accountability to stakeholders.

It is the libertarian fantasy: avoid the rabble, and get rich fast. This *is* liberation – but only for a charmed few, who can cream the benefits off their societies while leaving the rest to shoulder the costs and responsibilities.

In my experience, islands attract several types of people. There are those who want to escape the rules – whether those rules involve paying taxes, or shunning criminal activity, or being transparent, for example – while others simply want to indulge their megalomania in places where those with the gold can make the rules. For the past fifty years, both types have gravitated towards island tax havens with their offshore secrecy, lax, anything-goes laws, and a pliant finance industry staffed by local people who walk in trepidation, keep their heads down and won't blow the whistle. The result has become, as a rueful Polish professional worker told me a couple of years ago, 'an island without morals'.

Visit Jersey and you'll see scores of bankers, accountants, lawyers and others all engaged in helping their clients escape tax in other countries. Outwardly, everything appears smart and respectably British; all contributing to what journalist Nicholas Shaxson calls 'the theatre of probity' that cocoons such places and covers up the stink. Jersey describes itself as an extension of the City of London, which is itself an island state physically located in Britain but politically, economically and socially disconnected from the rest of the country.

Working in offshore finance in Jersey the 1980s I discovered that most of my clients were engaged in criminal or corrupt activity, including insider trading, market rigging, bribery, illicit political donations, tax evasion and avoidance. This happened behind complex structures of offshore companies and trusts, supported by a sophisticated pinstripe infrastructure of qualified professionals. Any preconceptions I had about corruption being something that happened in another country were turned on their head when I found that major British banks, law firms and accounting practices were up to their necks in it.

With few exceptions, my colleagues were indifferent to the impact of their work on the populations of other countries. They were aggressive, and in it for the money. Personal conversations seldom strayed beyond local gossip, cars and house prices. Once, when I raised an awkward question to my section supervisor about a client who was clearly embezzling Nigerian state funds, she told me, in characteristically blunt terms, that she didn't 'give a shit about Africa'. She was more brutally honest than most, but her hedonism and self-absorption epitomised the culture of most tax havens I have visited. Meanwhile hundreds of billions of dollars of African wealth spills out from the continent every year through British tax havens, with the active collusion of British banks, accounting firms and lawyers.

Look at any list of tax havens and you'll see that not only do islands feature heavily, but many fly a variant of the Union Jack and carry the Queen's head on their postage stamps. This is no coincidence. Since the 1950s the City of London has quietly spun a 'spider's web' of satellite tax havens which scoop up money, much of it dirty or abusive in one way or another, from around the world and funnel it discreetly through to London, the world capital of Capital. Britain's reassuring, ask-no-questions presence in the background is the stable bedrock that gives skittish global financiers the confidence to operate in Jersey's enclaves of turpitude.

In November 2013 I wrote to Her Majesty asking her, in her capacity as head of state of many small island tax havens, including the British Crown Dependencies (Guernsey, Jersey and the Isle of Man) and British Overseas Territories (such as Bermuda, the British Virgin Islands or the Cayman Islands), to request her prime minister to take all necessary steps to close down their tax haven secrecy functions. Britain controls these places, allowing some local democracy but retaining the power to strike down their laws at will, if it so chooses.

In her reply to me the Queen noted that her position as a constitutional sovereign precludes her from intervening in such matters, though a quiet word in the prime minister's ear at their weekly meeting would surely nudge him in the right direction. Indeed, David Cameron has publicly promised to lead the way by tackling Britain's tax havens, and in September 2013 went as far as to claim that 'I do not think it is fair any longer to refer to any of the Overseas Territories or Crown Dependencies as tax havens'. Spin and nonsense. Two months later, in November 2013, an exhaustive investigation by the Tax Justice Network's Financial Secrecy Index project revealed these jurisdictions as amongst the world's largest providers of financial secrecy services; and in December 2014 Christian Aid and Global Witness did their own joint investigation and reported very little progress in this area.

I left Jersey in 1998, leaving behind my home, my job, my friends and my island. It was an extraordinary wrench, not least because I had my own fantasy of how the island could have been a test bed for progressive social and environmental ideas. It never happened: the island remains captive to a plutocratic elite who are detached from ordinary Jersey people but use the island to pursue their own global ambitions.

The twenty-first century provides us with a worrying prospect. In country after country, privileged elites – the fewer than 1 per cent – are steadily peeling themselves away from any sense of attachment to nation states. Instead of contributing to the societies that feed their fast-growing wealth they float above or flit between nation states, creating their own island enclaves and gated communities. And yet despite their detachment from our societies, these elites seem increasingly to be controlling our politicians and political parties.

If we want to understand this new age of plutocracy, we need to talk about islands.

*John Christensen directs the Tax Justice Network (www.taxjustice.net). From 1987 to 1998 he served as Economic Adviser to the government of Jersey.

Bush Theatre

The Bush Theatre and Caroline Horton & Co with China Plate present

ISLANDS

by Caroline Horton

Commissioned by Warwick Arts Centre and Harlow Playhouse
15 January–21 February 2015
Bush Theatre, London

Islands has been developed in consultation with specialist economic advisers including John Christensen of the Tax Justice Network. Funded by Arts Council England and kindly supported by the Unity Theatre Trust and developed with the support of Oxford Playhouse, the Peggy Ramsay Foundation, NT Studio and South Street Arts Centre. Developed through Fuel's Jerwood Residencies at Cove Park, which are supported by the Jerwood Charitable Foundation.

ISLANDS

by Caroline Horton

Cast (performed and devised by the company)

Agent	**John Biddle**
Swill	**Seiriol Davies**
Mary	**Caroline Horton**
Eve	**Hannah Ringham**
Adam	**Simon Startin**

Creative Team

Writer	**Caroline Horton**
Director	**Omar Elerian**
Designer	**Oliver Townsend**
Lighting Designer	**Jackie Shemesh**
Sound Design	**Elena Peña**
Original Songs and Music	**John Biddle & Seiriol Davies**
Additional Lyrics	**Caroline Horton**
Additional Composition and Arrangement	**Elena Peña**
Assistant Director (BBC Fellowship)	**Lucy Skilbeck**
Script Consultant	**Selma Dimitrijevic**
Costume Supervisor	**Antonia Day**
Production Manager	**Ethan Hudson**
Stage Manager	**Jennifer Hunting**
Production Electrician	**Nic Farman**
Specialist Economic Adviser	**John Christensen, Tax Justice Network**
Tax Installation Coordinator	**Miquel Martinez-Pascual, Warwick University**

A special thanks from the company to Jean Andersson, Battersea Arts Centre, Ego Arts, Tamara Astor, Birmingham Rep, Hannah Boyde & Ben Adams, Hannah Bevan, Tom Booth, Anne Bourgeois Vignon, Gail Bradbrook, Tim Brierly, Matthew Broome, Matt Burman, Stan's Café, Gez Casey, Lizzie Wort & Chand Martinez, John Christensen, Simon & Christina Hicks, Adam Cohen, Clare & David O'Hara, Marianne Dicker, Gina Duckett, Poppy Faren, Frontseat Media, Linda Gatfield, Fionn Gill, Anna Glynn, Caroline Gonda, Gay & Jamie Graham, Nicola Graham, Vicky Graham, Anna Himali-Howard, Debbie Hollinshead, Tammy Holmes, Paul & Sally Horton, Emma Jarvis, Ed Jaspers, Caroline Jones and everyone at Action Aid, Delyth Jones, Mike Kaloski-Naylor, Gary Kitching, Dave Lipsey, Pat Lucas, Angie & Lydia-May Cooney, John Luther, Charlotte MacDiarmid, Brian McAuley, Michael Molloy, Mick Moore, Alex Murdoch, Richard Murphy, Liz Nelson, Alexandra Newsom, Daniel Pitt, Peggy Ramsey Trust, Nicholas Shaxson, Stage Sound Services, Geoff Southern, NT Studio, Alex Swift, Fuel Theatre, Tim Scorer, Annabel Turpin, Steve Voake, Gilly Wadmore, Michelle Walker, Lily Williams.

A heartfelt thanks to performance sponsors Rafael and Anne-Helene Biosse Duplan. Special thanks also to Ian & Hannah Alexander and Chris Watson for their kind support.

Finally, a huge thank you to South Street Reading, Cambridge Junction, Live Theatre and Warwick Arts Centre for their invaluable support throughout the development of the production on tour.

CREATIVE TEAM AND CAST

Writer | **Caroline Horton**

Caroline is a theatre maker, performer, writer and director based in Birmingham. She was nominated for a 2013 Olivier Award for Outstanding Achievement in an Affiliate Theatre for *You're Not Like the Other Girls Chrissy*, which also won Best Solo Performer at the 2010 *Stage* Awards. Caroline's second show *Mess* continues to tour after opening at the Traverse in August 2012, where it won Best Ensemble at *The Stage* Awards. *Mess* also won an Argus Angel award and was nominated for an Offie for Best New Play. In 2014 Caroline created and performed *Penelope Retold* for Derby Theatre, which tours the UK in Spring 2015, and her first radio play for BBC Radio 4, *Paris, Nana & Me*, shortlisted for the Imison Award. Current projects include creating a new show about the Staffordshire Hoard with the New Vic. She's an associate artist at Birmingham Rep and has just finished a year's residency at the Oxford Playhouse on their Evolve programme. She mentors the Rep's young theatre makers and is a regular workshop leader. Caroline regularly collaborates with other companies.

Director | **Omar Elerian**

Omar is Associate Director of the Bush Theatre. He is an Italian/ Palestinian theatre director, deviser and performer, trained at Jacques Lecoq International Theatre School in Paris. He moved to London in 2009 after having lived for six years in France, where he worked internationally as a freelance theatre practitioner. Working across art forms and styles, he has collaborated with artists and companies throughout Europe and the UK. His most recent directing credits include *You're Not Like The Other Girls Chrissy* (Edinburgh Festival and Bush Theatre), the acclaimed site-specific production *The Mill – City of Dreams* (Bradford, Yorkshire), *Testa di Rame* (Teatro Fortezza Vecchia, Italy), *Les P'tites Grandes Choses* (Maison de Arts du Cirque et du Clown, France) and *L'Envers du Décor* (Theatre Les Enfants Terribles, France). He was also Associate Director on Jericho House's *The Tempest*, which premièred in Palestine and Israel before opening as part of the Barbican's *BITE '11* season in St Giles Cripplegate.

Designer | **Oliver Townsend**

Oliver's designs includes *Dick Whittington and His Cat* (Lyric Hammersmith), *The Gamblers* (Greyscale), *Grounded* (Gate), *Dead to Me* (Greyscale), *The Art of Dying* (Royal Court), *Incognito* (nabokov, Bush), *The Blackest Black* (Hampstead), *No Place to Go* (Gate), *Rodelinda* (Scottish Opera), *Macbeth* (Blackheath Halls Opera), *Hitchcock Blonde* (Hull Truck), *Blood Wedding* (Royal & Derngate), *Gods Are Fallen and All Safety Gone* (Greyscale), *Wittenberg* (Gate), *Fings Ain't Wot They Used T'Be* (Union), *The Barber of Seville* (Opera Up Close). As costume designer his credits include *The Measures Taken* (Alexander Whitley Dance Company), *Wozzeck* (English National Opera), *The Lighthouse* (ROH Linbury), and *Big Maggie* (Druid). Oliver was the Winner of Best Set Design for *Grounded* at the 2013 Off West End Awards. He is an Associate Artist of the Gate Theatre, Notting Hill.

Lighting Designer | **Jackie Shemesh**

Jackie is a designer of lighting and space. He works internationally in dance, theatre, music and with performance and visual artists. Jackie has designed for many theatre productions in the UK including *The Ramayana* for Lyric Hammersmith and Bristol Old Vic, *The Hound of the Baskervilles* for Neal Street Productions at the Duchess Theatre, West End, *The Beloved* for Young Vic, Bush and Shiber Hur, *As You Like It* for Curve, Leicester, *The Penal Colony* and *Oh My Sweet Land* for the Young Vic. Most recently in London he worked with choreographers Hetain Patel, Ben Duke, Alexander Whitley, Colin Poole and Simon Ellis. Jackie has designed lighting for many dance companies including Batsheva Ensemble, Ballet Boyz, Introdans, National Dance Company Wales, Scottish Dance Theatre, CanDoCo, Protein and Yasmeen Godder. Other collaborations around Europe include the Hamburg Symphony Orchestra, Steirische Herbst Festival Austria, The JRMIP Congress in Berlin, Susanne Sachess and action collective CHEAP, and several projects with artists Yael Bartana, Phil Collins and Dana Yahalomi.

Sound Designer | **Elena Peña**

Elena's sound design credits include *The Meet Cute* (BBC Radio 4), *Seochon Odyssey* (HiSeoul Festival, Korea), *Patrias* (Edinburgh

International Festival), *The Kilburn Passion* (Tricycle), *The Wardrobe* (Tricycle/NT Connections), *The Girl's Guide to Saving the World* (HighTide), *Not Now Bernard* (Unicorn), *Macbeth: Blood Will Have Blood* (China Plate), *Pim & Theo* (NIE/Odsherred Teater, Denmark), *Yes, These Eyes Are the Windows* (Art Angel), *The Littles Quirky, The Muddy Choir* and *What the Thunder Said* (Theatre Centre), *A High Street Odyssey* (Inspector Sands/NT Watch This Space), *Flashes* (Young Vic), *Arabian Nights* (Tricycle), *Mass Observation* (Almeida), *Brimstone and Treacle* and *Knives in Hens* (Arcola), *Twelve Years* (BBC Radio 4), *Gambling* (Soho Theatre), *The 13 Midnight Challenges of Angelus Diablo* (RSC), *Quimeras* (Sadler's Wells, EIF), *Unbroken* (Gate), *Plasticine* (Southwark Playhouse) and *Under Milk Wood* (Northampton Theatre Royal).

Assistant Director | **Lucy Skilbeck**

Lucy is co-director of Milk Presents Theatre Company and the BBC Fellow for Derby Theatre. Credits as a director include *3 Wise* (Hiccup Theatre) and *Penelope Retold* (Derby Theatre). For Milk Presents: *Milk Presents: Self Service, A Real Man's Guide to Sainthood, Bluebeard: A Fairytale for Adults* (Total Theatre Nomination) and Young Vic SEN Festival (collaboration with Tangled Feet, Look Left Look Right and the Young Vic). As Associate Director her credits include *Father Christmas* by Raymond Briggs (Lyric Hammersmith, West Yorkshire Playhouse and Pins and Needles co-production). As an Assistant Director Lucy's credits include *The Odyssey* (Derby Theatre), *Encourage the Others* (Almeida Projects) and *Epidemic* (Old Vic New Voices). Lucy trained at the Royal Central School of Speech and Drama.

Script Consultant | **Selma Dimitrijevic**

Selma is Artistic Director of Greyscale, a Newcastle-based touring company. As a director and writer, Selma and Greyscale work with venues and companies nationally and internationally, including Northern Stage, Gate, Almeida, Dundee Rep, Tron and Camden People's Theatre. Recent works include *The Gamblers* (Greyscale/Dundee Rep), *Gods Are Fallen* and *All Safety Gone* (Greyscale) and *Dead to Me* (Gary Kitching and Co.) Her plays have been performed in the UK, Croatia, Russia, Ukraine and Canada.

Agent | **John Biddle**

John's theatre credits include *The Nutcracker* (Nuffield, Southampton), *Heidi: A Goat's Tale*, *The French Detective and the Blue Dog*, *Alice through the Looking Glass* (The Egg, Bath), *My Mother Told Me Not to Stare* (Theatre Hullabaloo), *Romeo and Juliet* (Night Light Theatre), *Alice* (Sheffield Crucible), *The Wonderful The Wizard of Oz* (Dukes, Lancaster), *We All Fall Down*, *The Shelter*, *The Ignatius Trail* (en masse theatre) and *Little Miss Jocelyn Live Shows* (Soho Theatre). Film and television credits include *Nan* (Old Trunk Media), *Peacock Season* (FMW), *The Amazing Dermot* (Channel 4). John's radio credits include ten series of *The Diary of Samuel Pepys*; *Paradigm*, *The Forgotten* and *In the Family* (BBC Radio 4), as well as several audiobook narrations for Audible. Credits as composer/musical director include *The Life and Times of Mitchell and Kenyon* (Oldham Coliseum), *Rift Zone* (Night Light), *The Queen's Knickers* (Southbank Centre), *The Gift and the Glory*, *Sabbat* (The Dukes, Lancaster), *Dracula*, *Wilde Tales*, *The Comedy of Errors*, *The Animated Tales of Shakespeare* (The Egg, Bath).

Swill | **Seiriol Davies**

Seiriol trained at London International School of Performing Arts. He is an actor slash writer slash composer. He's won some awards, including an Oxford Samuel Beckett Theatre Trust Award with Boileroom for *The Terrific Electric*, a *Stage* Award with Caroline Horton for *Mess*, and a Song for Wales Special Prize for a song about a small girl fighting evil with a gun that is actually a banana. He has worked with companies like Punchdrunk (*The Black Diamond*), You Need Me (*Certain Dark Things*), Gideon Reeling and Beady Eye (*Cooking Ghosts*). He is half of a time-travelling knees-up comedy act called Underbling & Vow. His new play *How to Win Against History* will première in 2015. It's a ripped-up musical about a fabulous cross-dressing aristocrat from North Wales, whose family burnt every record of his life after he died.

Eve | **Hannah Ringham**

Hannah is a co-founder and performer of the UK award-winning theatre collective SHUNT (Peter Brook Empty Space, Time Out Live, Total Theatre Awards among others), whose productions include

Dance Bear Dance, *Tropicana*, *The Architects*, the platform arts projects 'The Shunt Lounge' which ran from 2006 to 2010 and most recently *The Boy Who Climbed Out of His Face* (summer 2014).

She has performed and toured nationally and internationally with Tim Crouch, Sound and Fury and The Clod Ensemble among others. For the year 2012 she worked as a performer and creator on a collaborative experimental theatre project *Cadavre Exquis* in Belgium, together with Kassys (Holland), Tim Crouch (UK), 'The Nature Theater of Oklahoma' (USA) and Nicole Beutler (Germany). She works as an independent theatre maker creating shows such as *Free Show (bring money)*, a collaboration with Glen Neath, which was part of the British Council Showcase 2011, performed at the Soho Theatre and had a national tour. Hannah was one of the Oxford Playhouse Evolve artists for 2014.

Adam | **Simon Startin**

Simon's theatre credits include *Now You Know* (Hampstead Theatre), *Sherlock Holmes in Trouble* (Manchester Royal Exchange), *The Tempest* (Theatre Royal), *Beyond Midnight* (Trestle), *Heelz on Wheelz* (Fittings), *Pericles* (London Bubble), *Hamlet* (Red Shift), *Bartleby* (Red Shift), *Tartuffe* (Mappa Mundi), *Fanny Hill* (Dukes, Lancaster), *The Fly* (Oldham Coliseum), *Waiting for Godot* (Tottering Bipeds), *Collateral damage* (Traverse), *Subterranean* (Traverse), *The Fall of the House of Usher* (Graeae), *Volpone* (Graeae), *Ubu* (Graeae), *The Changeling* (BAC), *Love of a Good Man* (Arts Threshold). TV and film credits include *Holby City* (BBC), *Doctors* (BBC), *Keen Eddie* (Paramount), *Dunkirk* (BBC), *Are You Looking at Me* (BBC), *Preserve* (Channel 4). Radio credits include *The In Touch Xmas Panto* (BBC) and *Blind Jack* (BBC). As a writer Simon is now on his fourteenth professional commission, five of which have been named in Time Out Critics' Choice. He has recently directed *Offending the Audience* at the Young Vic and *A Midsummer Night's Dream* for the RSC. He has also lectured in Applied Theatre at Goldsmiths, University of London.

Bush Theatre

We make theatre for London. Now.

The Bush is a world-famous home for new plays and an internationally renowned champion of plays. We discover, nurture and produce the best new playwrights from the widest range of backgrounds from our home in a distinctive corner of west London.

The Bush has won over 100 awards and developed an enviable reputation for touring its acclaimed productions nationally and internationally.

We are excited by exceptional new voices, stories and perspectives – particularly those with contemporary bite which reflect the vibrancy of British culture now.

Now located in a recently renovated library building on the Uxbridge Road in the heart of Shepherd's Bush, the theatre houses a 144-seat auditorium, rehearsal rooms and a lively café bar.

bushtheatre.co.uk

Bush Theatre

THANK YOU
TO OUR SUPPORTERS

The Bush Theatre would like to extend a very special Thank You to the following Star Supporters, Corporate Members and Trusts & Foundations whose valuable contributions help us to nurture, develop and present some of the brightest new literary stars and theatre artists.

LONE STAR

Eric Abraham
Gianni Alen-Buckley
Michael Alen-Buckley
Garvin & Steffanie Brown
Siri & Rob Cope
Alice Findlay
Miles Morland
Lady Susie Sainsbury
James & Virginia Turnbull
Mr & Mrs Anthony Whyatt

HANDFUL OF STARS

Anonymous
Rafael & Anne-Helene Biosse Duplan
Philip & Tita Byrne
Clyde Cooper
Irene Danilovich
Catherine Faulks
Kate Groes
Christopher Hampton
Simon & Katherine Johnson
Emmie Jones
Paul & Cathy Kafka
Pierre Lagrange & Roubi L'Roubi
Eugenie White & Andrew Loewenthal
Charlie & Polly McAndrew
Aditya Mittal
Paige Nelson
Philip & Biddy Percival
Joana & Henrik Schliemann
Philippa Seal & Philip Jones QC
The Van Tulleken Family
Charlotte & Simon Warshaw
Hilary & Stuart Williams

RISING STARS

ACT IV
Nicholas Alt
Anonymous
Melanie Aram
Nick Balfour
Tessa Bamford
Jim Broadbent
David Brooks
Lord & Lady Burlington
Maggie Burrows
Clive Butler
Matthew Byam Shaw
Benedetta Cassinelli
Tim & Andrea Clark
Sarah Clarke
Claude & Susie Cochin de Billy
Carole & Neville Conrad
Matthew Cushen

RISING STARS CONTINUED

Liz & Simon Dingemans
Andrew & Amanda Duncan
Lady Antonia Fraser
Rosie & Richard Gledhill
Global Cause Consultancy
Jack Gordon & Kate Lacy
Richard Gordon
Hugh & Sarah Grootenhuis
Thea Guest
Lesley Hill & Russ Shaw
Madeleine Hodgkin
Bea Hollond
Sarita Jha
Ann & Ravi Joseph
Davina & Malcolm Judelson
Kristen Kennish
Nicola Kerr
Sue Knox
Adrian & Annabel Lloyd
Isabella Macpherson
Penny Marland
Michael McCoy
Judith Mellor
Michael Millership
Caro Millington
David Mills
Tracy O'Riordan
Georgia Oetker
Kevin Pakenham
Denise Parkinson
Mark & Anne Paterson
Barbara Prideaux
Emily Reeve
Sarah Richards
Robert Rooney
Sir Paul & Lady Ruddock
John Seal and Karen Scofield
Jon & NoraLee Sedmak
John & Tita Shakeshaft
Diane Sheridan
Saleem & Alexandra Siddiqi
Melanie Slimmon
Brian Smith
Nick Starr
Ed Vaizey
Marina Vaizey
Francois & Arrelle von Hurter
Trish Wadley
Amanda Waggott
Olivia Warham
Peter Wilson-Smith & Kat Callo
Alison Winter
Andrew & Carey Wright

CORPORATE MEMBERS

LEADING LIGHT

Winton Capital Management

FOOTLIGHT

Innocent

LIGHTBULB

The Agency (London) Ltd

SPONSORS & SUPPORTERS

Kudos
MAC Cosmetics
Markson Pianos
Oberon Books
The Groucho Club
The Village at Westfield London
Waitrose Community Matters
West 12 Shopping & Leisure Centre

TRUSTS AND FOUNDATIONS

The Andrew Lloyd Webber Foundation
BBC Performing Arts Fund
Coutts Charitable Trust
The Daisy Trust
The D'Oyly Carte Charitable Trust
EC&O Venues Charitable Trust
Foundation for Sport and the Arts
Garfield Weston Foundation
Garrick Charitable Trust
The Gatsby Charitable Foundation
The Goldsmiths' Company
Hammersmith United Charities
The Harold Hyam Wingate Foundation
The Idlewild Trust
Japan Foundation
Jerwood Charitable Foundation
The J Paul Getty Jnr Charitable Trust
The John Thaw Foundation
The Laurie & Gillian Marsh Charitable Trust
The Leverhulme Trust
The Martin Bowley Charitable Trust
Royal Victoria Hall Foundation
Sir Siegmund Warburg's Voluntary
Settlement
Sita Trust
The Theatres Trust
The Thistle Trust
The Williams Charitable Trust
The Worshipful Company of Grocers

PUBLIC FUNDING

If you are interested in finding out how to be involved, please visit the 'Support Us' section of www.bushtheatre.co.uk, email development@bushtheatre.co.uk or call 020 8743 3584

China Plate is an independent theatre studio that works with artists, venues, festivals and funders to make original, exciting theatre that often plays with form and always has narrative at its heart.

The company achieves this through three strands of work:

- **Developing** (artist development and commissioning)

- **Making** (origination and touring)

- **Programming** (seasons, festivals and events)

China Plate work with a number of the UK's most exciting artists and are currently making work with Caroline Horton, Action Hero, Chris Thorpe, Contender Charlie, Dan Jones and Inspector Sands. *Islands* is the third collaboration between Caroline Horton and China Plate (previous award-winning work includes *Mess* and *You're Not Like the Other Girls Chrissy*).

China Plate are Associate Producers at Warwick Arts Centre where they develop and commission new work, Artistic Associates at the New Wolsey Theatre where they are Directors of PULSE Festival, Programmers of New Directions (the NRTF showcase), and producers of innovative development programmes including The Darkroom, The Optimists training programme and The First Bite and Bite Size Festivals.

China Plate are **Ed Collier, Paul Warwick, Kirsten Burrows and Iain Goosey.**

chinaplatetheatre.com

facebook.com/chinaplatetheatre

twitter.com/YourOldChina

vimeo.com/user9631729

warwick arts centre

Warwick Arts Centre is one of the UK's largest and most outstanding presenters of contemporary live and visual arts. *Islands* marks a continuation of their long relationship with Caroline Horton and as a supporter of her work, having previously developed *Mess* as part of the Triggered@Warwick programme.

It aims to be a place of creative stimulation, refreshment, and artistic adventure for audiences and artists alike; and is one of a small group of significant presenters and co-producers of contemporary performing and visual arts outside London.

Based at the heart of the University of Warwick in Coventry, our vision is to present and produce outstanding work by artists of both international standing and with exciting reputations.

For more information on Warwick Arts Centre, visit warwickartscentre.co.uk

HARLOW PLAYHOUSE
CREATE · ENJOY · FOR ALL

Harlow Playhouse is a leading creative centre in the East of England, creating and presenting a programme of high-quality theatre, music, comedy, dance and circus arts; engaging the communities of West Essex and East Hertfordshire.

It aims to nurture arts projects, companies and artists within the Eastern and national landscapes, providing commissions, rehearsal space and production support for a wide range of activities. Harlow Playhouse is a cultural service provided by Harlow Council.

For more information on Harlow Playhouse, visit playhouseharlow.com

Islands

Islands – the making of
by Caroline Horton

Following the financial crisis of 2008, I realized how little I understood about how our economy functions. Like many others, I started wading through the proliferation of books that explain in layman's terms how the system is supposed to work and 'what had gone wrong' from people like Michael Lewis and John Lanchester.

But it was the glimpse into the world of offshore finance that spun me into new realms of disbelief. I developed a macabre fascination for these little worlds where big business and high-net-worth individuals were able to make up the rules to suit their own ends – via a network of law and accountancy firms. Very early on in my research, I wrote to John Christensen of the Tax Justice Network about my ideas. His support and input have been invaluable – together with Nicholas Shaxson's brilliant *Treasure Islands*, which John suggested I read after our first animated Skype conversation about *Islands*.

Also, I really like islands, especially small ones: pictures and photographs of islands draw me; I love the fantasy they offer of being away from the real world, with a huge buffer of sea surrounding me and things feeling simpler. Of course, tax havens are not all palm-fringed islands – though it's fascinating how many of them are. But from Delaware to Luxembourg to Jersey to the City of London – each of them behaves as if there was a great ocean permanently dividing them from the rest of us.

As my research continued, I began to understand the human rights abuses that exist as a result of offshore. Previously, I'd not connected tax evasion and aggressive tax avoidance with anything other than 'people not paying their fair share' – but the human cost became increasingly evident. The abuse comes via many channels – whether through tax havens hiding 'dirty money', or capital flight from developing countries into tax havens, or multinationals hindering developing countries from building their own tax base by siphoning money into offshore, or simply the fact that if the wealthiest sections of society avoid tax, everyone else has to pay more while services (and everything else) are cut, and inequality continues to increase.

Violent aggression towards the rest of the world is hidden beneath offshore's façade of respectable business – the lawyers, accountants, nice offices, talk of wealth creation and easing international trade.

It was offshore's aggression – the real human cost of avoiding tax and the grotesque level of greed – that stood out to me as I started to think about making a show.

Islands, like other shows I've made, has been created through a devising process. I realised, however, that with this subject matter I was going to need to write much earlier in the process than I usually would – if only to avoid an hour and a half of show about how complex and confusing offshore finance is. So after some short bursts in a devising room, I went away and wrote a great sprawling draft that we then used as a jumping off point for further improvisation. The script was refined and reworked in the room with gaps in between rehearsals where I could go away and rewrite.

We've drawn from a grotesque, physical form – 'bouffon' – that I studied at Ecole Philippe Gaulier. These creatures, society's outcasts, come to mock and rabble-rouse. We have of course just taken what was useful to us from the bouffon world – this is by no means a study in form. Something really valuable was offered in the bouffon spirit, however – their ability to be wickedly funny and foul, yet also epic and deeply political.

I was interested in trying to make a show where we told a big story, translating the concept of offshore to the realms of gods; I didn't set out to explain the mechanisms and schemes through which offshore operates. I wanted to see if we could connect audiences with offshore and tax evasion beyond an intellectual recognition that it is unjust. I wanted to see if the underbelly of it could horrify us.

I hope the show is a good night out – and a trigger for debate and further exploration of the issues raised.

I'm completely indebted to the brave and wonderful team I've worked with throughout. Here's to a big, exciting leap of faith!

Note on the text: As with any play, the script only captures the text and some of the visual language, but here so much of the play's spirit exists outside of the language, the script can only give an indication of the show in performance.

On the edge of the world the landscape is desolate, something like an abandoned pool or abattoir. Junk including an old toilet and some plants. In one corner, an old diving platform (signs read 'Don't Climb', 'Keep Off'). Walls covered in plastic sheeting. Audience seats arranged on four sides around a central, tiled pit with sluices and drains visible.

Mary, *foul and friendly, enters eating cherries – smiling through her grime – singing sometimes – and definitely up to something.*

Mary (*climbs to top of her diving platform. Text along these lines*)   Life is just a bowl of cherries. Doo doo be doo. (*Her mouth is full of fruit.*) Hmmm. Want a cherry? I definitely washed them. Hello. (*Dribbling.*) Whoopsiedaisy. Beg my pardon.

Looks about her and grins, speaks into mic from top of platform.

Good evening, a very good evening, an excellent evening. Thanks for coming. My name is Mary – I'd ask yours but it'd take too long. Apologies for the mess, (*looks about*) this world we live in . . . be nice to get away, wouldn't it? Once, when I was fourteen, I shut myself upstairs in my bedroom for a month. I put a padlock on the door; graffitied the walls with felt-tips; smoked Lucky Strikes in bed; watched *Betty Blue*, *Silence of the Lambs* and *Friends* videos over and over; got drunk on Strongbow; melted biros; dyed my hair blue; lived off Cadbury's Fruit & Nut and Lucozade; masturbated a lot; experimented with eyeliner; and refused to communicate with 'them' downstairs. They shrugged, rolled their eyes, thought I'd gone nuts. Hadn't. It was heaven – my room, my rules, none of their shit – like I wassa little god.

Let's say . . . let's say yamma a little god. Just for fun. And as god, let's say I'm upgrading . . . relocating . . . expanding. This time I want an island and so no one can interfere, my island's gonna rip itself free – free from the poor and shitty chaos – and orbit the world – that I'm renaming Shitworld. Just for fun, harmless fun.

*Blows whistle – gang jog in and round. Like Mary, they are have-
nots and misfits – androgynous, terrible looking, full of mystery.
Their eyes shine with mischief, wickedness, watchfulness.*

Agent   Hi, Mary.

Swill   Hi, Mary.

Eve   Hi, Mary.

Adam   Hi, Mary.

Mary   Agent? (*He stops.*) Swill? (*He stops.*) Demonstrate my
island orbiting Shitworld. (**Swill** *runs.*) Faster, Swill.
Thanksyou. What else?

Swill   Buildings! Big ones!

Mary   As tall and as glorious as my holy pen-ise.

Agent   And crunchy gravel for the Rolls-Royce to drive over.

Mary   Yes and everyone on Shitworld is gonna stare up at
us in the sky and, quite naturally, start to worship us.

Swill   And we'll be awash with aplenty etc.

Mary   Well let's do that then.

Agent   Now all we need is a bit of Shitworld to call our own
then launch into the sky.

Mary   No problem when you're a god. (*Whistle.*) Swill, we
got it. So one day, this holiest of trinities (**Agent** *and* **Swill**
pose.) spots Adam (*Whistle call,* **Adam** *in position.*) a simple
freelance gardener and Eve (*Whistle call,* **Eve** *in position.*) his
charming, ambitious wife on their patch of Shitworld.

Adam *makes tea, then reads gardening magazine. Lovely domestic
scene. Loo, plants, chair (later used by DJ* **Swill**) *and a rug too.
Little radio. The trinity watch.*

Adam   Tea, Eve? I'll be done by four-ish – just a couple of
lawns to see to, bit of pruning.

Eve   I'll do us soup then. Leek and potato ok?

Mary   If you get bored . . . add the word 'fun' – in your
head, not out loud.

Eve   Adam, the reminder for the gas bill's come.

Adam   Wasn't raining when you went out – was it? Eve?

Eve   No.

Swill (*whispers*)   Fun.

Eve   I saw the deer again – from the end of the garden.

Adam   That's good then.

Swill   Fun

Adam   Good good.

Heads to loo – sits for a while, then waves empty loo roll at **Eve** *who hands him a new one.*

Mary   Knock knock – so sorry to disturb.

Eve   Hello.

Agent   Pleased – to – meet – you.

Mary   We're the gods. Don't get up.

Swill   Swill.

Agent   Susan, Jane, Agent – call me Agent.

Mary   Mary.

Adam   I'm Adam – this is Eve.

Eve   Pleased to meet you.

Mary   Howdus feel bout an invasion-slash-upgrade?

Adam   What?

Eve   Where?

Mary   Here Shitbuckets, a friendly takeover, perks aplenty – here's a cuntract.

Throws **Eve** *a glittering high heel.*

Adam   Can I say something?

Mary   Of course. You'll be 'honorary governors' . . . sounds flash n'est-ce pas?

Adam   Can I say something?

Swill   Yes. Do you dance, honorary governor?

He initiates rough, sexy tango with **Adam**. **Eve** *and* **Mary** *head to top of pool steps.*

Mary   Eve – (*leads her up pool steps*) we've cherry-picked you and your bit of Shitworld.

Agent   This is your chance. What do you smell, Eve?

Mary   She smells shit, Agent.

Agent   Exactly but she's used to it isn't she?

Mary   Buses, queues, savers baked beans. Let's leave it behind, Eve – let's fly.

Agent   Up there, Eve – wow – oh wow the heights.

Swill *humps* **Eve** *delicately. She giggles, then shrieks, enjoying it.*

Agent   How do you feel, Eve?

Eve   Oooh wow woooo wow – the heights!

Adam   Is this procedure?

Swill   We're all friends here, Adam.

Agent   Let's vote. In favour?

Mary, **Agent**, **Swill**, **Eve** *raise their hands.*

Adam (*raises hand*)   Can I say something?

Mary   Carried.

Fantasy music plays – like an advert for a gated community in Dubai. **Adam** *and* **Eve**'s *belongings are scattered or adopted for use by the trinity.*

Swill   And this was the beginning of the new kingdom. At god's command, our humble plot ripped itself free – free from the poor and shitty chaos of Shitworld – up we floated – up and up . . .

Mary   And I did name my floater . . . Haven!

'Haven' sign lights up, grand SFX.

Swill   On the seventh day, safe in orbit at approximately thirty feet, we did obliterate ourselves on happy hour cocktails and passed out.

Agent (*indicates platform wreathed in fake cherry blossom*)   At some point one of us did manage to plant a tree . . .

Mary   Like that other god did back in the day 'cept mine's a cherry tree. Moresexculsivo. Duntyaknow.

Agent (*looks down central drain to Shitworld beneath*)   Look at them. So many of them. You could soar like us on eagle wings if you'd just get up off your lazy arses. May we inspire you Shitworld and may we have a lot of fucking fun above your heads. Merci. Amen.

Mary   God's commandments. Ten. Ten is traditional.

Agent   Please be aware:

– Characters, places and events have no basis in reality so any resemblance to persons living or dead is purely coincidental.

– Information is of a general nature and is in no way meant as a substitute for professional advice from an accountant.

– We cannot be held responsible for acts of god.

Swill (*evangelist voice*)   One – thou shalt not pinch Mary's cherries.

Mary   Hands offa my fruit.

Swill (*evangelist voice*)   Two – gods shall go immediately to the front of the queue for everything.

Mary   Especially queues for ice cream, sushi and hookers.

Swill (*evangelist voice*)   Three – don't scratch. She hates it. Four . . .

Mary   That'll do. Hope that's all fair and fabulous? Good'oh. Open for business.

Adam *stands clutching the remaining item from his home – his loo.*

Agent   Fabby. Sign sign and sign.

Trinity *make their sign.*

Mary (*to audience*)   Everyone ok so far? All ok?

Swill   Wanted to check you're ok so far . . . You look ok.

Agent   If we're all ok so far that's ok then.

Trinity *and* **Eve** *head up the steps.*

Adam (*to* **Mary**)   Should we bend over and let you fuck us up the arse as well . . . Anyone for Pimms with their free hump?

Mary   Sorry about him. Etiquette, Adam. Really sorry.

Doorbell rings. First cherry delivery. Deliveries arrive as if through a dumb waiter. Carefully mimed journey of doors and switches.
Trinity *sing first version of 'Who's got all the cherries? Uh-huh uh-huh.' First package is a jiffy bag collected by* **Agent***. Cherry juice spills from it on route to locker.*

Swill *dashes to swivel chair. 'On Air' sign lights up.*

Swill   Ping pong ding dong, lads and lasses: it's Haven's voice of choice, this is MC Swill on 99.99 Radio Free-de-de-de-dom 'Put on your condom, this is freedom'. Hands up if you love freedom. That's great. I can't actually see you because I'm on the fucking radio, but I assume slash hope every hand is in the air now because – come on! Freedom! Oh yeah – now some motivational mojo – bless us all – it's my godfathers. Uh!

He lip syncs to the voices of Friedman, Reagan, Thatcher.

'The world runs, on individuals pursuing their separate interests. Once you, once you, once you stop those wealth creators, from creating the wealth, then there's nothing e-e-extra to distribute. The great achievements of civilisation have not come from government government bureaucrats.

Being free to choose should be every person's birthright.
Everywhere in the world we need to keep government on
the sidelines. Let the people develop their own skills, solve
their own problems, better their own lives (lives lives).'

Swill   A look at the weather: it's nice, featuring the sun and
several degrees, and looking to get more nice throughout
the rest of the week slash our lives. So well done us. Here's a
song called 'Fly Like an Eagle', which I like because I like
eagles, and also would like to be an eagle. This one's going
out to you if you would similarly like that. Go be an eagle.

Mary *takes mime gun from* **Agent** – *chooses largest from proffered
selection. Shoots eagle. Song stops.* **Agent** *positions* **Adam** *to collect
the dead eagle. Relaxing music plays.* **Eve** *and* **Mary** *on top step out
of pool.*

Agent *and* **Mary** *(sung)*   Take me to Haven

Eve   Mary . . .

Swill *(sung)*   It's not on the map

Agent *and* **Mary** *(sung)*   Bring me to Haven

Swill *(sung)*   It's not not on the map

Eve   Is it not? Is it not on the map?

Agent *and* **Mary** *(sung)*   Let's go to Haven

Swill *(sung)*   It's not not not on the map

Eve   Mary . . .

Agent *and* **Mary** *(sung)*   We live in Haven

Eve   Mary . . .

Trinity *(sung)*   It's not not not not illegal
   It's not not not not illegal
   It's not not not not illegal
   Cos its paradise, paradise
   It is very very very . . . nice

Eve   Mary – how did you become a god? I want to learn. I'm just sixteen going on seventeen waiting for life to start. Oh look – a squirrel – a red one – rare nowadays.

Mary *fires –* **Swill** *does SFX.*

Eve   Can I – can I do that?

Mary *hands her the gun – SFX don't work, instead the gun says 'good evening'.*

Mary   It's complicated, Eve.

She fires.

Eve   God god. Don't patronize me. I'm not just a dumb blonde. I'm an ambitious young woman with real drive.

Mary *heads towards Paul on the platform – he's a pink bust-phone, who's been blindfolded and taped up.*

Mary   We're the frontier Eve. Pushing the envelope, etc.

Eve (*scratches*)   But what do you do? . . . The cherries are important right?

Mary   Don't scratch. (*Music cuts.*) Catechism time. How can you glorify god?

Eve   By loving her and doing what she commands.

Mary   Good girl.

Swill   Where is god?

Eve   God is everywhere.

Agent   Does god know all things?

Eve   Yes.

Mary   Can god do all things?

Eve   Yes.

Mary   Then best fear god and serve her faithfully with all your heart, n'est-ce pas?

Eve   So just to be clear, what do you . . .

She scratches.

Mary   EVE! . . . Don't scratch and don't bore these people.

She climbs up, music restarts. Pops Paul on her knee and picks up receiver.

Eve   Oh right – sure. Just to reiterate I'd be happy to help with the cherries . . . in whatever way . . . picking, baking, pickling, cleaning up? Mary . . . Mary?

Mary (*on phone*)   Hi, Paul. So, lovebird, how's things at Shitworld HQ?

Swill/Agent   Hi, Paul

Eve   Who's Paul?

Mary   What's that? What can I see? Well, my darling, I can see my houses. (*To audience.*) How many houses do you have? One? I have nineteen. Plus a camper van so nineteen and a half really.

Eve   Can't I come up? Mary? Mary?

Mary   What's that, my darling? Cars? Yes I can see my cars. (*To audience.*) Do you have a car? Well done/never mind. I've got a mini – convertible, a range rover, a lambrini, an HGV and double decker bus (red with my own bus driver). That down there is my fifty-foot yacht and my fourth wife is sat on the deck – 'Hello, Gloria' – Russian model. Nice tits. (*Back to Paul on phone.*) Plan for the day? Oh just the euge-yaknow – lunch at 1 – sushi and Ribena – afternoon nap – managing of managerially complex MBWA management by wandering around – self-glorification at 4 – tea on a trolley at 6 then watch porn and listen to *The Archers* (*To audience.*) (you can get it online abroad nowadays) and bed with a husband at 11. Beauty sleep is key. Don't work too hard. Ta-ta treacle.

Eve (*jealous*)   Who's Paul?!

Mary   Oh we go way back – me and Paulie – I remember the day he knocked on my door . . .

Agent   Knock knock – my name's Paul.

Mary   Says he's from Shitworld Government HQ and starts asking all these questions. Private information he's wanting – top secret. So while I think . . . I ring for scones (scones) and tea. I say – let's play a game, Paul, and if you win, I'll open up the filing cabinets, unlock the vaults, hand over the big black box, give you whatever you want. We tied his arms and legs together. Turned off the lights. More romantic.

Eve   Did he win? . . .

Mary   No no . . . But it all worked out splendidly in the end.

Eve   Where's Paul now?

Swill   Back at his desk – he gives us a ring every now and again from Shitworld HQ – keeps us up to date.

Agent   Paul's key isn't he? Really key . . . a lynch . . . pin.

Eve   I could be too – one day – maybe I could be key too?

Mary   As key as Paul? Listen to this, Eve – we'll start you at the bottom, with the cubicle monkeys . . . but if you work hard . . .

Agent   Like a dog.

Swill   Woof woof.

Mary   Then who knows . . .

Eve   Wow. Brilliant. Don't mind getting my hands dirty.

Agent *hands her the gun. SFX work this time.*

Mary   Good shot, Eve. Bravo.

Trinity (*sung*)   Cos its paradise, paradise
  It is very very very . . .

Eve   . . . nice

Delivery two of cherries. **Swill** *collects. A dripping briefcase.*
Trinity *sing a more elaborate 'Who's got all the cherries?'* **Mary**

pauses by **Adam** *and his loo. He's hidden himself behind a wall of plants.* **Adam** *hums softly 'doom boom . . . lala'.*

Mary   Hello, the workers. How do you like the new arrangements? Settling in ok? . . . What's that one then?

Adam   Narcissus poeticus.

Mary   Looks like a daffodil to me.

Adam   It is. Watch your step.

Mary   We're alike you and me, Adam – don't like to be interfered with. (**Mary** *kicks over a pot.*) My cherries are thriving. A cherry year's a merry year.

It's now darkened to a gloom. **Swill** *dashes to radio chair. 'On Air' sign. 'Joy to the World' plays. Other four gather for Christmassy tale.*

Swill   Ding dong merrily oh hi everybody: Haven calling. Archbishop MC Desmond Swill here, with the daily service from the cathedral of Haven. We are currently cruising at 35 feet above Shitworld. Now call me an old, handsome softy if you want, but I'd like now to gather round the fire and share with you this festive story of giving; it's one of my favourites. It's called 'The Christmas Capitalist'.

He lip-syncs to neo-liberal do-gooder clip.

'I wanna share with you errm . . . an experience I had . . . so we're blasting out Christmas music driving round the slums . . . erm and every so often . . . we'd stop and just hand out these gifts . . . sometimes we couldn't come to a complete stop . . . erm . . . so yeah we just . . . threw four or five gifts out through the open window . . . erm yeah . . . and I tell you . . . these kids . . . a few of them did a great job catching those gifts . . . that I threw at them . . . and it got me thinking . . . I mean . . . when I think about all the laws we'd be breaking . . . if we did that in the so called 'civilised' world . . . it's crazy.'

Oh wow, that story got me wet in both eyes. Here's a legendary track by the supergroup Band Aid: a band, of course, that's a literal who's who of people who gathered together for a greater good: Bob Geldof, One Direction, Bono, Bananarama, Milton Friedman, Margaret Thatcher, Bono again, Simon Le Bon and Ayn Rand on glockenspiel. Take it away, guys . . .

Ends with short clip of 'Heal the World!' Gang joins in. **Mary** *climbs up to platform and blows whistle.* **Eve** *starts step-ups. Manic edge to her – pace builds. She moves to a different section of audience on each whistle from* **Mary**. **Adam** *is endlessly offering* **Eve** *tea from his flask. She pushes the cup away more and more violently.*

Adam   Would you like a cup of tea?

Eve (*pushes tea mug away*)   It's exciting – isn't it, Adam – progress? New home – smaller, more expensive but more exclusive. Up up and away. I feel taller, actually taller.

Adam   Eve?

Eve (*to a very close audience member*)   New neighbours here. Hello. Hello. Maybe we'll be friends or just acquaintances. Who knows! We'll sensitively work out what's ok and what's not. What's friendly, also what's weird etc, . . . like . . . like . . . I'm wondering do you believe in god . . . a god? And what do you do? Are you in a relationship? I'm not asking – not yet – it's private. (*Whispers – something aggressive surfaces.*) I want to ask you loads of personal questions because I'm interested, I'm really, really interested but I won't – 'no need to panic'.

Adam   Would you like a cup of tea?

Eve (*talks faster and faster – pushes tea away*)   Tut tut 'don't scratch, Eve'. Etiquette. Yes! Know all about it I do. That's how we keep order. (**Mary** *blows whistle –* **Eve** *moves –* **Mary** *blows whistle – workout restarts.*)

Eve   – Don't talk over the top of other people.

– Don't talk about shit or sex or cum at the dinner table. Oh no! Haha.

And whatever happens don't mention cash. Do not mention cash.

Mary *blows whistle to stop* – **Eve** *moves* – *whistle to restart workout.*

Eve   Cash cash bucks dollars pounds pence cents euros balances. How much do you earn? What do you get? And who's winning? (*Steps faster.*) Who?!

Adam   Eve – have a . . .

Eve *bangs tea away.* **Mary** *blows whistle to signal* **Eve** *to move.* **Agent** *and* **Swill** *jog with her, dab her with towel, spray water until she restarts on* **Mary**'s *whistle.*

Eve   Don't you want more than this, Adam? More than your shit-pay-never-enough-work-freelance-gardening?

Adam   Eve . . .

Eve   When the gods arrived didn't you think 'lucky us', 'glowing prospects'? I did. Bam – she gives me a job – ha! You could get one too, Adam – a proper job.

Adam   I've got a job.

Eve   It's not worth shit, Adam.

Mary *blows whistle to signal* **Eve** *to move.* **Agent** *and* **Swill** *jog along with her, dab her with towel, hand her water until she restarts on* **Mary**'s *whistle.*

Eve   My first morning god teaches me to snip the names off the accounts before I file. And it's boomtimes for Adam and Eve – rubbing my hands . . . First pay cheque's in – 'I'm getting us a car, Adam . . . boom – our own car!' 'Gal you're-on-ya-way hey-hey!' Oh the island life for me. Speedin my heart up to a better speed. Screwing my sleep down to a littler slice. Fun fun rush rush.

Adam   Have some tea.

Eve   I'll have a whiskey.

Whistle from **Mary**, **Swill** *and* **Agent** *stay with* **Eve** *now.* **Eve** *scratches.*

Eve   Sometimes wonder who the people are I'm chopping off and popping in the wastepaper?

Mary (*on mic*)   Don't scratch, Eve.

Agent *and* **Swill** *step away from* **Eve**.

Eve   Whoops. Once – got muddled doing the adding up (*Scratches.*) – 'God, I can't seem to make the numbers work' . . .

Mary (*on mic*)   Go back to the spreadsheet, Eve.

Eve   Penny drops . . . let the magic happen – don't scratch! Not expected to understand the minutiae am I? The gods bark with approval. (*Gods bark for fun.*) Oh the hills are alive!

Adam (*yells over the top*)   Eve! Drink your tea!

Eve (*music soars in underneath*)   I've set up the Julie Andrews Appreciation Society, Adam – I re-enact *The Sound of Music* once a month – keeps me out of trouble.

Trinity (*sung*)   It is very very nice!
   We live in Haven.

All spread arms wide. **Eve**, *exhausted, collapses onto mattress.*

Mary   Are you having a lovely time?

Swill   Isn't it lovely?

Agent   Wanted to check you were having a lovely time.

Mary   We are. Everso.

Adam   I am.

Eve   All lovely – a lovely time.

Agent   Lovely. So thought we'd play our favourite game.

Swill   You'll love it. It's lovely.

Game show theme music, light show.

Mary   Welcome to 'Play Dirty'. Good, clean fun for all the family.

Trinity *greet the audience.*

Swill   Please welcome your host and deity – it's Mary, everyone!

Applause SFX.

Mary   Thank you so much. May I introduce my lovely assistant –

Swill   Swilla –

Mary   – and my other lovely assistant –

Agent   Susan, Whitney, Susan.

Mary   How will our honorary governors fare in tonight's dirty economics challenge? The stakes are high, ladies and gentlemen, here on 'Play Dirty' . . . a winning score changes the law.

Cheers SFX.

Swill   Wow. Real. Life. Law.

Mary   I'm so excited I could piss myself. Let's meet the contestants.

Agent   Eve – office worker and founder of Haven's *Sound of Music* appreciation society.

Cheers SFX.

Swill   And her devoted husband and gardener – Adam.

Applause SFX – **Mary** *immediately ends it.*

Mary   Contestants, it's in your hands. We don't have to tell you how much this means. If you triumph, the new laws will protect Haven and her cherries from the grubby and indeed shitty fingers of Shitworld HQ. What's on the legal list today, Susan, Whitney, Susan and Swilla?

Agent   Well, Mary, first off we have brand new secrecy laws: including trusty trust laws to protect Haven's privacy from the nosey parkers on Shitworld. That's trust.

Mary   Trust you.

Agent   Trust you more.

Swill   Secondly we've got brand new freedadeedadeedom laws so Haven can launch a fasbulous totes unregulated market trading sexclusively in 'cherries'.

Mary   Not cherries of course but 'cherries'.

Swill   Exactly, Mary – so we can be as carefree and 'risky von whisky' as we want without Shitworld incessantly shouting 'stop it'.

Agent   And finally we have some brand new holes and legal loopdaloopholes so Haven can wriggle out of whatever regulations Shitworld throws at us.

Mary   Got all that, governors? Wow – incredible – more cherries for 'everyone'. What the fuck's wrong with that in the name of politeness?

Agent   Assistant Swilla, let's administer the red tape.

Swill *and* **Agent** *wrap* **Eve** *and* **Adam** *together in the centre.*

Mary   How are you feeling, governors? Studied economics at school by any chance? (*Shake their heads.*) Not your fault then. Niche subject that barely affects us in the real world.

Agent   Cherryconomics challenge.

Mary   Clench your butts and here we go.

Exciting quiz music begins. **Trinity** *shine torches on governors.*

Agent   Eve. We have three – lets call them – crabs.

Swill   Fresh.

Mary   How many crabs?

Eve   Three.

Swill   Notional total?

Eve   Three?

Mary   Wrong, Eve – twelve – look to the future.

Agent   Adam. We give away four notional crabs.

Swill   And we receive an actual seventeen from you. I now have how many crabs?

Adam   Twenty-three crabs

Swill   Correct.

Mary   I drop twenty-four crabs leaving us with a negative crab, which wanders sideways towards a crab pot. What does that mean?

Adam   Nothing.

Agent   Almost, Adam. Coming to you, Eve . . .

Eve   Crab for tea? I like crab? Watch for the shell?

Mary   Focus, Eve.

Agent   I'll repeat the question – it took me a while to invent this system so I understand why you are struggling to take it all into your thick skull.

We have three crabs, we give you four notionally, one of them gives birth actually.

Mary   She's a single mother so gets extra credit.

Swill   Three-fifths of tiny crabs die and we get a loan to pay for the vet to visit.

Agent   We now have twelve crabs – you get to hold a notional five and for the privilege give us seven back.

Mary   We now have nineteen notional crabs.

Swill   Eve, how many crabs do *you* have?

Eve   Ummmm.

Mary   We're almost out of time, Eve.

Eve   Six . . . is it? I think it might be . . . no no . . . magic . . .
600 crabs.

Mary   I need your final answer.

Eve   A cast of 600 crabs.

Timer SFX ends.

Mary   And we're just waiting for the independent judging
panel . . . oh yes that is the correct answer. And the one we
adore will tell us the score.

Agent   Well, Mary, the honorary governors have a score of
three trillion cherries meaning . . .

Mary   Laws passed. (*Cheers SFX.*) Congratulations!

Swill   Incredible. Freedom rings out.

Eve   It's a miracle.

Mary   God loves a miracle. Is that the time? You've been
such a lovely audience. See you again soon on 'Play Dirty'.

Theme music plays.

Agent   See you at the office tomorrow, Evie.

Swill   Wow. You really saved the day there, Eve.

Mary (*heads off singing softly – arm around* **Eve**)   It's only a
game show.

Mary *and* **Eve**   It's only a game show.

Adam   Can I say something? This is a joke.

Mary   No, Adam. Game show. Have you not understood?

Adam *pushes a crate over, it falls with a crash. Ringing signals
delivery of cherries.* **Mary** *raises her hand, no one moves.* **Adam**
and **Mary** *eyeball.*

Mary   I wish it was different too. Take a look, Adam, through the godseye . . . Everyone's doing it. Everyone's at it. Like rabbits.

Hops daintily to mic. She then sings jazz song in her most charming voice.

> If you come upstairs to the Hob Nob Club
> You'll find a door the colour of blood;
> Come on inside, take the easy chair
> And I will come and visit you there
> And what is my name, did I hear you ask?
> The Devil. Wearing a Mary-mask.
> If you really want the pain to end
> Take some advice from your new best friend,
> Sit on your hands, discard all your plans,
> Pay your subscription and join the dance.

She signals the change – driving music on piano and cello. Darkness. Hellish. To **Adam** *as he looks down into the drain.*

Mary   Stay up here where you belong
> The folks who live below, they don't know right from wrong.
> So stay up here where you belong
> We can't extend your membership unless you sing along.
> So kick up those heels and have some fun,
> You haven't really lived until you've stared into a gun.
> But don't open up the members' book;
> The key to seeing clearly is to know where not to look.

Adam *closes the drain cover. Ringing reminds us there's a delivery of cherries waiting.*

Mary   Ding dong! Ding dong! It's for you, Adam. Ding dong . . .

Adam *collects delivery – larger package, more cherry juice drips. He gets his hands bloody for the first time.* **Eve** *goes to help him or just follows behind and sings softly in a whisper of encouragement 'Who's got all the cherries'.*

Mary   It's all a rotten shame isn't it, Adam? Going to start a revolution? Head out into the world and take yourself on a march.

Trinity *sing more elaborate version still, 'Who's got all the cherries? Uh huh uh huh.'*

Agent *has a fag.* **Eve** *gets a drag sometimes.* **Swill** *has some small sandwiches.* **Mary** *eats cherries. They have a break.*

Agent   I went on a march. Several.

Swill   I went on one once too.

Eve   Oh wow.

Swill   Good to march.

Eve   Stretches the legs.

Agent   The last one I went naked.

Swill   I crawled on my belly like this.

Agent   Oh me too me too. Because I care.

Eve   I care too.

Swill   I scratched my nipples along the ground.

Agent   I did too – til the points fell off.

Adam *and* **Eve** *gradually build towards full-on teenage groping session.*

Eve   Well done

Adam   I love you.

Eve   Adam, ssssh.

Adam   I'd march for you.

Eve   That's nice.

Adam   I love you. Want to erm?

Eve   I have to go to work.

They stumble offstage for a quickie in the delivery area. At some point, **Adam** *re-enters, straightens his clothes and sits in audience with rich-tea biscuits.*

Mary   There are three stages to a bullfight. Beforehand . . . they keep the bull in the dark; starve him; dose him with laxatives; stick knitting needles in his genitals; push cotton wool buds up his nostrils and blind him with Vaseline. They tend to let the door slam on his head as he runs out into the ring. So stage 1 – the Picador – man on horse who stabs bull with triangular pronged weapon – bull goes nuts and gores the horse to death or near death. Each time a horse's insides need stuffing back in – we pause – they use a handful of hay to stop it all sloshing about – then stitch him up. Picador rides a horse til it actually drops dead. Know why the horses don't scream? Because someone slices through their vocal chords before the fight – well a screaming horse would put the punters off. Stage 2: the Bander-ill-ero comes out – great outfit he has plus a selection of harpoons that he stabs into the bull's muscles – so the bull's running round like some massive porcupine. Then finally – stage 3 – the matador – with his red cape – he darts around so the porcupine bull gets crazier and crazier and weaker and weaker until the matador finishes him off by stabbing him in the heart – except often he misses his target and punctures the lungs so the bull's spewing blood and then – the guy starts hacking at the spinal column to paralyse the bull so it at least looks dead. They drag it out the back and the knackerman starts skinning him but if it's not quite dead yet – the bull jumps up and tries to run away. Six or seven bulls fight over three to six hours watched by sixty thousand people. Legal some places. Mankind's extraordinary – don't you think? I'd like to see it – beginning to end. Wonder if I'd puke. I suppose because the killing is shared, one feels less guilt. (*To an audience member.*) You look a bit green. Think about Mickey Mouse or something.

Fade to very different lighting state – time has passed. **Adam** *is sprightly – makes it ever so romantic (dim light, easy listening music* *medley plays), scatters some rose petals, sits, waits, grinning.* **Eve** *arrives from deliveries entrance – she's soaked, holding a bloody, dead deer in a car blanket. Blood is on her hands, face. The gods watch.*

Eve   Sorry I'm late.

Adam   Surprise!

Eve (*looks down at deer under coat*)   . . . I didn't see it coming.

Adam   Righty-ho. (*Whistles.*) You're soaked.

Eve   It's raining.

Adam   Tea?

Eve   I was driving on the cliff road.

Lights flicker, burst of gurgling from drain.

What was that?

Adam   Nothing. Fancy a biscuit?

Turns up easy listening music.

Eve (*lights flicker, burst of gurgling*)   Again – listen. (*Tries to scratch.*) He made such a noise against the car, then slid off the bonnet. I couldn't . . . in case he wasn't quite . . . so I just stood at the cliff – we're flying low, Adam – why are we so low? (*Tries to scratch.*) I was going to move him to the side of the road. But when . . .

Adam   You've had a shock. (*Whistles.*)

Eve   Shut up.

Lights flicker, burst of gurgling, she flinches, acknowledges, scratches. Whispers – the gods are watching.

What's in those packages, Adam? Is it cherries? It is cherries, isn't it?

Looks at her bloody hands.

Adam   Cherry market's booming!

Eve   I feel sick.

Retches.

Adam   You're a good girl, Eve – try not to scratch.

Eve   Why? Why's that?

Adam   How can you glorify god?

Eve   By loving her and doing what she commands.

Adam   Where is god?

Eve   God is everywhere.

Adam   Does god know all things?

Eve   Yes.

Adam   Can god do all things?

Eve   Yes.

Adam (*looks at deer*)   Put it with the rubbish eh?
    Tell you what . . . tell you what . . .
    In the Garden of Eden sat Adam,
    Massaging the bust of his madam,
    He chuckled with mirth,
    For he knew that on earth,
    There were only two boobs and he had 'em.

Eve *stands with deer.*

Incredibly long fart noise from central drain. **Agent** *pulls mass of disgusting hair out of drain. News bursts through.*

Agent   'At one point the market fell as if down a well. We're down by between 3 and 4 and a half per cent. We are red everywhere essentially, down by 4, 5 per cent. We are down 9 per cent. Cyprus is nearly broke, the social fabric is beginning to tear. Paris market down by 9 per cent. Austria is down by nearly 11 per cent. We're down over 16 per cent. Has fallen about 18 per cent. The stock market is now down 21 per cent. We're now down 43 per cent. What in the world is happening on Wall Street?'

He shoves hair in drain. **Swill** *dashes to radio – does his penetrating Jeremy Paxman voice.*

Gang play serious news-time game. Purposeful walking and stern faces.

Eve *carries deer to edge of space – stays staring at it, at her red hands, freezes a moment before returning to the edge of the pool. She stays slightly numb – tries to join in – hobbles about on her one high heel.*

Swill   Good evening, and this is the news. My name is Moira Swillert, good evening. We interrupt the normal flows of today to bring you this abnormal and serious bulletin that is breaking now . . . now. (*Important jingle.*) Today, Shitworld's economic tits have gone up: economies are tumbling, people are defaulting all over the floor, and absolutely everybody is using this tone of voice. Latest reports claim that Shitworld is crawling around on its hands and knees in agony emitting really bad farts. Shitworld markets today opened so far down they were stinky and brown but who is to blame? We go straight over all serious now to our on-the-ground correspondent Gloomy Lemons. Gloomy, where are you?

Agent (*lying on the ground in audience*)   I'm on the ground, Moira.

Swill   What's it like?

Agent   Sticky.

Swill   And?

Agent   Uncomfortable.

Swill   Terrifying. What can you hear?

Agent   Well, Moira, serious noises that imply important events and the sense that something has really, genuinely happened here.

Swill   Can you speak to anyone?

Agent   Yes, people won't stop talking: it's quite annoying.

Swill   And?

Agent   Everyone is poor and surprised. Here's one now. Hello, sir, what do you want to say today? (*Mic held up – loud crying SFX.*) Thank you. This is Gloomy Lemons on the ground. Back to you, Moira.

News music returns.

Swill   Thanks, Gloomy. The closing headlines today, DONG: Super economic death-farts on Shitworld. (*All DONG.*) Northern Cock and the Peeman Brothers have gone totally A over T fucking up all the money. (*All DONG.*) Everyone's got no job now. (*All DONG.*) The scabby faces of Shitworld are united in asking their governments, their banks: (*'Where's all our money gone? Where's all our money gone?' SFX and weeping.*)

Agent   God had a heartfelt message from Haven.

Mary   Shitworld, with tears in my eyes, I reach out to you – to the shattered, to the penniless, to the confused pensioners whizzing from bank to bank on their mobility scooters. Haven is poised to launch an in-depth, internal investigation – on us by us – in case we can help provide even the smallest clue as to what the fuck happened to you poor twats. We're fine up here thanks for asking.

Agent   In-depth, internal investigation. Go.

Launches SFX for internal investigation.

Mary   Chase me. Manhandle me. Tie me down.

Agent   Nice cop?

Swill   Ver sorry – sozzles but erm . . . where's the money?

Mary   I don't know. I'm perfect.

Swill   Dammit she's good. Bad cop?

Agent   You look like a foreskin in hell. Good cop?

Swill   You look lovely. Have a biscuit. Bad cop?

Agent   You've left me with no choice. We going in. Open up, Mary.

Mary   I'm warning you dammit – I know my rights.

Swill   Trim the foliage.

Agent   Slash through the thorny forest.

Adam   Open the flaps.

Swill   Yum. Cheesey dip?

Agent   Don't make a fist of it now.

Adam   What's that noise?

Mary   It's angry – it's making a cracking sound.

Agent   I see – it's trying to throw me off the scent. Where's the goddam sheriff when you need him?

Adam   Sir, are you the sheriff?

Mary   Are you my lawyer?

Swill   I am the independent fanny ombudsman. I take very little pleasure in my work.

Shines torch and speaks into echoey mic between **Mary**'s *splayed legs.*

Swill   Stalactites, stalagmites. Cavern. Yes, I would like to know where the money is. Hello – it's Mr Tumnus. And friends.

Adam   Has he got the stolen cash?

Swill   Tumnus, I'm warning you . . . Come back here. What's that down your trousers? Ah I see. Well done. (**Swill** *gasps for air.*) Well, chaps – no snifter of a threepenny bitcoin. Her havenly kingdom is clean.

Paradise song a cappella – **Eve** *joins in 'it is very very very, really very, oh so cherry, merry cherry, bloody Mary nice'. All fall into pile on mattress. Night. Pile of bodies on/around mattress – some snoring.* **Eve** *peels herself out of the pile of bodies – woken by the* *itching. Tender moment moving* **Adam**'s *hand from her – gently places it back down. Has to pass close to audience round pit to get to the loo.*

Eve   Scuse me scuse me. Sorry sorry.

Opens loo – looks – pulls cherries clumped with hair out of the toilet. Loud gurgling erupts. Looks for where to leave the disgusting clump. Gives it to an audience member. She sits.

Don't mind me, just gonna . . . (*Sound of weeing, relief.*) Sorry, sorry.

How much did you pay for your seat then? . . . Enjoying it? (*Farts.*) Sorry.

She just sits and looks. Looks about for loo roll.

Haven't got a tissue have you? Sorry.

Either thanks them or says don't worry and shakes bum. Goes to flush – there isn't one.

No flush.

Itching grows worse, she struggles not to scratch. Physical battle.

(*Stands looking at the cherry tree.*) 'Surely ye shall not die the day ye eat thereof . . . your eyes shall be opened, and ye shall be as gods.'

She gives in and scratches furiously.

Just a couple? (*Eats a single cherry.*) Hmmm. (*Eats another.*) Hmmm. 'Ye shall be as gods!' Good-oh.

She grins and stands over the drain cover – eats cherries – more and more – cramming them into her mouth – stuffs cherries more and more slowly until she's completely still.

Opens drain cover – stares in. Freezes. Spits cherries out – retches. Drone builds. Goes to cherry packages – opens lockers, pulls lids off, rummages in cherry juice – pulls out her red arms. Noise, **Adam** *wakes – he tries to stop her.*

Adam (*hushed*)   Eve . . . Eve . . . you mustn't.

He shuts drain. **Eve** *reopens it.*

Eve   What did you see, Adam – through the godseye?

Adam   Nothing.

Eve *looks at her arms – revolted, scratches.*

Adam   Eve.

Eve (*offers her arms, horrified*)   Look, Adam.

She smells juice, retches.

Adam   Cherries.

Eve (*practical*)   Adam, we have to leave now.

Adam   Ssssh, Eve.

Eve (*shouts*)   AH! Turn all to blood . . . The gods are in reverse . . .

The gods wake. **Adam** *retreats.*

Eve (*practical*)   Adam, get your things.

Tries to take deer – **Trinity** *block her.*

Mary   The cherries were forbidden, Eve – the rules remember. Rules are important.

Eve   Come on now, Adam – quickly please. (*Scratches.*)

Eve *now by door,* **Mary** *between* **Adam** *and* **Eve.**

Mary   Don't scratch, Eve. Last chance . . . quiet now and we'll talk.

Eve (*scratches*)   NO – Eve will not be quiet. NO. And back down on Shitworld – I will not be quiet. In the shitty streets, I will not be quiet. Eve will scratch and scratch and scratch and one day when . . . you will pay.

Mary   Out of my sight, Eve – out.

Eve *to dumb waiter, followed by* **Swill** *and* **Agent**. *Drone pounds.*
Mary *closes drain and advances on* **Adam**. **Adam** *takes half a step towards the dumb-waiter door. We hear it leave.* **Agent** *and* **Swill** *re-enter.* **Mary** *leaves* **Adam** *to cower. The gods look at one another.* **Mary** *starts storm – huge thunder and lightning; wind and rain; sound of drains; huge base chord drones beneath.*

Mary   EVVVVVVEEE. Eve. Crack crack ber no frensaya taredsawre EVE EVA EVAAAA. Ah Ah. Ganferd rost depacha ho ho kolnmer tret. Tret crackber. (*Signals more thunder claps.*) Silopena vornatcher quando cherinde veno qand. Hikledo hikledo Evie eva. Non non wakin sund fastay di frica di dia di glendan sicrak. (*Sees* **Adam** *in the corner.*) Coy coyde oj laben labente. Eveee. Leto. Letonde.

Mary *stops once exhausted, emptied.*

Agent (*translates* **Mary** *for us*)   Eve. Eve. Because thou hast done this, I will greatly multiply thy sorrow . . . thou art cursed above all cattle. Eve Eva. Thou shalt eat dust all the days of thy life . . . Bring me her heart, I will salt it and eat it . . . remember, Eve . . . dust thou art, and shalt unto dust return.

Mary (*quite calm*)   Adam. When she calls . . . let us know . . . won't you? . . . How she's getting on . . . Ask her, Adam, I want to understand, ask what she lacked up here? . . . What she could possibly have lacked . . . What's she up to Adam – down there with the multitudes? . . . Ungrateful slag. (*Sudden intake of breath.*) Perhaps she's you know . . . (*'Mental', 'deranged' gestures.*) Poor Eve. She's not thinking of (*Blows her whistle repeatedly.*) . . . is she? Not a good idea I'd say. What, Adam? Got something to say?

Adam   'doom boom doom boom . . . doom boom doom boom'.

Mary   Anyone else want to go? No problem if you do. We'll close our eyes. Count to ten . . . 1, 2, 3, 4, 5, (*Gurgling grows.*) 6, 7, 8, 9, 10.

Gurgling increasing. Lights flicker. **Mary** *still boiling – dons ear defenders,* **Swill** *does the same – they play with an inflatable globe.* **Agent** *arms self with plunger, goggles.* **Adam** *follows helpfully.* **Agent** *listens to toilet, central drain, sluice gates. Clearing drains – each of which emit farts, gurgles and unpleasant news flashes from Shitworld – he then re-plugs.* **Agent** *opens the toilet lid:*

Voice of Barack Obama   'We're gonna shut down those offshore tax havens and all those corporate loopholes you shouldn't have to pay higher taxes because some big corporation cut corners to avoid don't pay their share.'

Agent *shuts the lid and opens it again.*

Voice of George Osborne   'The swift and decisive action of in year cuts and emergency budgets . . . We have created an internationally admired, respected and independent office for budget responsibility. These bold steps have made Britain that safe haven in this sovereign debt storm.'

Agent *unblocks the SL sluice gate with a wrench.*

Voice of protestors   '. . . pay your tax or we will shut you down! Starbucks pay your tax / or we will shut you down!'

Agent *blocks the sluice gate again. He removes the lid off the central drain. Unblocks with plunger.*

Voice of David Cameron   'The agenda we have is one that is about helping the world to grow together. Making sure we crack down on tax evasion . . .'

Agent *replugs drain.*

Voice of David Cameron   '. . . and aggressive tax avoidance, (**Mary** *and* **Swill** *look up.*) so right across the world, countries get the tax revenue needed (**Mary** *and* **Swill** *lift one ear of their headphones off – start to replace.*) to keep the taxes . . .

Mary *and* **Swill** *take off their headphones.*

Mary   Sounds fruity this morning. Do you need a hand?

Agent   No, no.

Mary *and* **Swill** *replace headphones.*

Voice of David Cameron   '. . . down for hard working people and to make sure we can have good health and education systems for all our people.'

Agent *places drain cover back.*

Mary (*shouting to each other*)   When did everyone get so pious? . . . I'm so bored . . .

Voice of Margaret Hodge (*bursts from the central drain*) 'We're not accusing you of being illegal; we're accusing you of being immoral.'

Agent *makes* **Adam** *block it with his hands.* **Adam** *struggles to keep central drain blocked, uses plunger.* **Agent** *berates him.*

Voice of Margaret Hodge   'Your covenant says you "do no evil" and I think you do do evil, in that you use smoke and mirrors to avoid paying tax.'

Spokesperson from Tax Justice Network (*pops out of various different drains and the toilet –* **Agent** *loses control*)   'The . . . 2020 have committed themselves to this . . . automatic information exchange . . . this must also be extended to, the, poorer countries of the world to ensure they are able to cut back on their own tax evasion problems . . .The more the governments try shifting the tax burden away from businesses and away from wealth holders, onto ordinary people, the wider the inequality becomes . . .'

Agent *blocks the toilet with* **Adam**'s *plant.* **Agent** *replaces* **Adam**'s *hand with a loo roll. Wipes own hands. Picks up Paul phone – goes through to voicemail.*

Agent   Hi, Paul. Look can you call me back, mate? Need an update on these rumblings from Shitworld. Want to check it's all in hand. Shouldn't you be at your desk dealing with this shit for us? Anyway, call as soon as you get this.

*Replaces phone. Phone rings loudly – 'Hey it's Paul, he blesses you'
ringtone –* **Agent** *answers.*

Agent   Hello? . . . Paul? I'll pop you on speaker phone.

Paul   This is rather awkward . . .

Agent   Not at all . . .

Paul   Got my Shitworld HQ hat on you see . . .

Agent   Good for you.

Paul   Well – post the 'crisis' . . . I presume you're aware.

Agent   Uh huh – we're pretty much ok up here.

Paul   Nothing you need to tell us?

Agent   As a child I was bullied? That sort of thing? Look,
Paul, old chum, what are you doing to sort these rebels out?
They're starting to piss us off.

Paul   Watch your tone, mate.

Agent   What?

Paul   Look – Lord Vanilla Smoothie. Monsieur . . . Cool
dude, etc. This is the real deal. We're clamping down on
offshore.

Agent   Haha – very funny, Paulie – I'm a bit busy though so
/ if you don't mind . . .

Paul (*booms over PA*) /   Is or is not Haven a fucking tax haven?

*The gods are struck down, convulse, each time tax is mentioned. End
crumpled on floor.*

Mary   Paul – don't use the T word it's like nails on a
blackboard.

Paul   Tax haven admit it.

Agent   No no – easy mistake to make but in fact we are a
pioneering, world-class, independent, / international centre
of . . .

Paul   Tax haven. Tax haven. Mary, take a look down that godseye of yours. You're cruising close to the shit my friend. Eve's been stirring and now everyone's pointing at Haven.

Mary *pulls open drain, sound of angry mob bursts out. She stares down into the light then slams it shut.*

Mary   I'd love to help but you'll just have to tell them I've really not a clue.

Paul   They know, Mary. They know you prevent Shitworld taxing the wealthiest companies and individuals because Haven hides their fucking money. Immoral and often illegal. There's blood on your hands, Mary.

Mary   That's cherry juice, ya dick.

Paul   Shut up about cherries and make some notes. Make some memos for a change. Get me signed tax information exchange agreements and beneficial ownership details by Pooseday or we'll end you. We need names ok? Account details, got me? Who benefits from the shell companies and trusts. Then Shitworld intends to tax the hell out of those lying cunts whose cash you've been sitting on. You lot better get so fucking transparent you're see-through. I'm setting my tomato timer now, Lady Mary – I suggest you do the same. (*He rings off.*)

Mary, **Agent**, **Swill** *look. Each press panic button/pull panic cords – deafening air raid siren sounds. Loud patriotic recording of 'Rule Britannia'. All four don different military hats. Listen from trenches.*

Swill (*avuncular DJ* **Swill** *voice*)   Good evening, Haven dwellers. Avuncular Churchswill here at (*Jingle.*) Freedom Radio. You will have heard the news from Shitworld. Dark times are upon us. Difficult times. Our current altitude is just 11 feet. But keep calm friends and wear a Keep Calm and Carry On T-shirt, or an amusing variant on that design, like Keep Calm and Eat Cupcakes, or something like that, that you think expresses you as a person. We will fight this thing. We will fight it on the beaches. We will fight in the nice fields and streets; in the organic bakeries and Nandos. And so take heart! Know that however hard it seems, however dark; Haven will remain floating nobly above the shit. Good night.

Agent   Operation bull. Three prongs. Like a fork. Prong one – 'Picador'. Arm yourselves, soldiers.

Crates and phone centre stage. **Adam** *acts as secretary.*

Mary   Get me Teddy. Hello, old thing. We're in the market for a little headline . . . Smashing.

Swill   Get me TB – Paul's old boss.

Mary   Lunch tomorrow? Cheeky martini or five beforehand. Perfecto. See you at 12.

Swill   Ding dong Haven calling. Haha! Where are you? On your hols? God soz to disturb.

Agent   Get me Paul's Mum. Chouchou – comment ca va? L'Agent ici – you may remember me from my time as Minister de Shitworld Cash. Oh you do? Formidable.

Swill   Wondered if you'd have a stern word with Paul over a bottle of pinot splendidot. Stunning. Ta-ta now.

Agent   Would you sit slightly too near the twat faction in Shitworld HQ whispering threats? Great.

Mary   Get me Paul's hooker. Bunny! What's up honey bun? I miss your pretty legs. Want to drop by?

Agent   Meanwhile I'll talk loudly about growth, competition and all those cherry-based jobs that contribute to Shitworld's economy, etc.

Swill   Get me Tubster. What's up bean? Be great if you could head up the think-tank division for us. So thrilled. Laters.

Agent   You know the score sexy, let's open that door.

Mary   Get me Sherlock. Sherlster? Have Paul watched.

Swill   Get me Stonker.

Agent   Get me Smuts.

Mary   Get me Toff.

Swill   Stonker you brute.

Agent   Smutters.

Mary   Toffles.

Trinity   One for all and all for one? Fabsters. (*Phones down.*)

Swill (*proffers phone*)   Get me an ordinary person.

Adam   Hi.

Swill   Christ – erm hi – yes so what do you think about the current situation? What can we do to help?

Adam   Say you're sorry and you won't do it again.

Mary   Fuck you.

Swill   Thanks so much ordinary person.

Adam   I like having a voice.

Agent   Prong two – (*Winks – clever code.*) 'Banderillero'. Right, Mary. You're on Bitchard and Doodoo tomorrow at 7.30 a.m. Adam – make it all nice. Chip-chop.

TV sofa arrangement. **Adam** *holds plant/air-freshener.* **Swill** *plays* **Bitchard**. *Doodoo on music box. Theme music.* **Mary** *takes her boobs off – smartens up . . .*

Bitchard   Joining us from Haven, it's Mary. Hi, Mary, well you're looking great despite some pretty negative press lately.

Mary   Hi, Bitchard. Hi, Doodoo. Thanks for having me.

Bitchard   Mary how did you get to where you are today? Haha. Such a heart warming tale. Hmm.

Mary   Thanks, Bitchard – I grew up on Shitworld's cold
northern streets – age twelve I was malnourished and all
yellow. I'm sorry. (*She weeps.*) Each day, I'd look myself in the
face – in a puddle cos we didn't have a mirror you see and
I'd say out loud – I am free – I am Mary – and one day I will
be Mary the great. A few years later Haven was born.

Bitchard   Do you feel able to respond to the shocking
accusations about Haven? I mean are we talking paradise or
parasite Mary?

Mary   That hurts, Bitchard. Let me take this moment to tell
you what Haven is – may I speak plainly? We are a world-
class, independent, internationally innovative centre of
excellence; a pioneering opportunity in a world struggling
to stay free. We are not engaged in illegal activity, we are
engaged in liberty, in free competition. These recent
allegations come from an unstable former employee. You
know me, Bitchard – I am soft, I'm lovable, but what I really
want to do is reach in, rip out Eve's heart and eat it before
she dies . . .

Agent   Cut cut. Go back.

Mary   You know me, Bitchard – I'm soft, I'm lovable, but
what I really want to do is reach . . . out to you, Eve – with an
arm of pity, an eye of sorrow, a leg of lamb, an olive. Haven
has pledged a voluntary contribution of valuable cherries to
help Shitworld out and we are listening – to you the public,
to economists, to Shitworld HQ, to the misled hippies lined
up against us. I'm a new listening god – more listeny and
additionally, also more transparent too meaning see-
through. Thanks so much for this moment, Bitchard . . .
Doodoo.

Bitchard   Thanks, Mary, moving stuff.

Agent   Prong three of our three pronged fork. Matador.
Let's have a thought-shower babes.

In the style of The West Wing – *march down corridors – some theme music.*

Swill   First off, Mr President – if they shut Haven – then what?

Agent   Just rename Haven? Newhaven? Shaven?

Swill   What about second citizenship, Mr President?

Agent   Or offshore underwater dwellings?

Swill   I know I know! Build a bunch of bespoke oil platforms? Call them sea-steads . . . as in home-stead but on the sea, Mr President.

Mary (*bursts into office, thinking positions*)   No one in their right minds would live on an oil platform.

Swill   There's always outer space I suppose. We gat spaceships don't we, Mr President?

Agent   A time machine, Mr President? Then we just travel back to the eighties.

Swill   Got it – we upload ourselves onto the internet, Mr President.

Mary   I'll just nuke Shitworld. I've done it before.

Adam   Can I say something?

Mary (*pause*)   Why not?

Adam   Mary . . . I mean Mr President – how about telling Shitworld 'Stop pointing at us and get your own house in order. Number one: sell sell sell – get rid – hospitals, schools, post offices, police – the lot. Two: stop giving cash and sympathy to immigrants, single mothers, ill people, artists and cripples – stop it! Three: raise taxes from the masses and learn how to collect them properly – stop being polite.' They need to stand up – man up – do it for their country. (**Agent**, **Swill**, **Mary** *slow clap*.) I like having a voice, Mr President.

Mary   Well done, Adam. They should just do that.

Swill   Yeah – they should probably just do that then.

Agent   We'll austere them in the right direction.

Mary   Hi, Shitizen.

Swill   Morning, Shitizen.

Agent   Hello, Shitizen. Tutututut.

Swill   How are you? Naughty . . .

Mary   Anything you want to tell us?

Agent   Cos we're closing in hmmm hmmm.

Swill   Just want to be sure you're not keeping anything to yourself.

Agent   If you've declared all you should . . . you've nothing to fear.

Mary   Show us what you're hiding, Shitizen.

Agent *and* **Swill** *play sexy music. Long pause.* **Adam** *steps centre stage and does a slow, bad striptease. He flicks into his burlesque number – unclear how complicit he is at points. In the style of Noël Coward, half spoken half-sung.*

Adam   Good evening. Hi – I'm hungry. Anyone got any food? Now we've all been very naughty and we have to be punished. My name's Austerity Measures. Delighted to be with you . . . for the foreseeable.

Swill *hands him a bower.*

Adam   We understand, we really do
    If only it was up to you
    Your hands are tied, no need to explain, boss
    I'm not one to complain, boss
    I know you thought of us, isn't that true?
    Never out of your mind as you furrowed your brow
    It's got to be done, no backtracking now
    Please don't feel guilt, love
    You'll make yourself ill, love

I'm sure you're thinking of us still
A spoonful of sugar like it says in that song (*Gang continue this part.*)
Helps the austerity medicine along
Don't worry about us – don't fret
We know very well that it's not over yet . . .
We'll get by for the good of this land
Though we're thin and it hurts us to stand
It's the least we can offer
To refill those coffers
And you'll think of us – won't you? . . .
And you'll think of us – won't you . . .

Timer goes off. Help dress **Adam**. *Mad panic about being ready for Paul. Mopping, tidying, careful arranging of cherry boxes. Cherries out in a bowl. Air freshener. SFX of threatening stilettos marching slowly down a corridor. Everyone smiling and ready/ 'we didn't do nothing' faces. Military formation.*

Paul (*SFX voice*)   / Pomodoro, time's up. Step away from the mop. Such damage, Mary (*She steps centre.*) – we've so much to rebuild. You say Haven acted within the law, but has this become a question of morality rather than legality? (**Mary** *goes to speak.*) SHUT UP. So you've signed the agreements, you're more see-through. You've made some big promises, Mary, but can you be trusted to stick to the new deal? Life's a bowl of cherries up here – but down there, they're sick of the pips. (*Tense* X-Factor *results-type music.*) Haven, I can now reveal . . . You're through to next week. Congratulations. You've warmed my cockles, Mary. Together, we've changed things. I feel truly proud of what we've achieved.

Mary   Me too me too.

Paul   Sssh. Take my advice – keep your heads down, low profile, etc. See you soon chums.

Bell rings signalling final massive cherry delivery. **Adam** *collects, walks packages round pool. Sings 'who's got all the cherries'. Conga slowly comes in over text and disco lights.*

Agent   Well that could've gone worse.

Mary   Well done us.

Swill   Haven is cruising once more at a safe height of 30 feet above the shit . . .

Mary   Under the circumstances. . ..

Agent   Shouldn't we mark the occasion? I could ring for tea . . .

Swill   Well Adam could do tea . . . If we're going to *ring* . . . should make it count.

Mary   Maybe a cream tea then.

Agent   Couple of scones (scones) maybe . . .?

Swill   With jam? Or just butter just butter.

Agent   Or maybe jam too – little plastic pot of jam?

Mary   Robertson's blackcurrant . . . Fancy a scone (scone) Adam? Just a little one.

Adam   I like scones.

Mary   And maybe if they have it, only if they do . . . some cream? Clotted? Or squirty's fine too.

Agent   I'll ask. Here we go . . .

Swill   Or maybe, as we did do quite well . . . a little glass of something . . .

Mary   Almost traditional with high tea . . .

Agent   Glass of fizz?

Swill   As there are three, sorry four, of us . . . best to get a bottle?

Agent   Works out cheaper.

Swill   Just one bottle.

Mary   Yes although economies of scale . . . probably cheaper to get a biggish bottle.

Adam   A jeroboam.

Agent   Adam! I would say yes. I'll check. Hello can I place an order please . . .

Swill (*music starts and keeps building*)   Although hold on a sec . . . I mean . . . we should probably make sure there's enough food you know . . . in case anyone else pops in.

Adam   Like hookers?

Agent   Adam. Naughty. They heard that.

Mary   Well if they heard. Just a couple?

Swill   Each – a couple each . . .

Adam   Beluga.

Agent   Adam! Sssh! Could just have caviar instead?

Swill   I was thinking, all this stuff . . . maybe we should just go out?

Mary   What ring for a little taxi?

Agent (*does aeroplane*)   A little taxi yes.

Swill   Just pop over dunno – maybe Miami or Ibiza just Ibiza?

Agent   Ibiza's on the way – so could do both? May as well.

Mary   What do you think, Adam?

Adam   Miami club plus hookers and miaow miaow.

Mary   Okey dokey – Adam's in the swing.

Agent   What about staff? At the club – we should have staff – but just a few – just some small staff –

Adam   Dwarves?

Mary Adam! Maybe import some from Mexico – much cheaper that way.

Swill Also to save on washing up – could ask them to lie down, spray their naked bodies with champagne and lick it off them.

Mary And food-wise I'm seeing nibbles plus a massive piñata – full of pick and mix and miaow miaow for pud.

Agent Could bash it open with one of the little tiny staff as they're there.

Swill Music-wise. Nothing OTT. Just a disco DJ?

Agent Maybe see if Calvin Harris is free?

Swill Failing that, Cliff Richard?

Mary Just the one song though – 'Congratulations' would seem appropriate.

Agent Then later on a little orchestra maybe? Or the Vienna Boys, Choir?

Mary Failing that, Riverdance? (*To audience.*) Chip in if there's anything we've missed? Anything you'd like?

Agent Hello? Hi there. I am placing an order for a little celebration. Ok scones (scones), champagne – a jeroboam was it, Adam? A really small private jet, hookers, staff that lie down . . . What else?

Adam Beluga.

Agent Oh yes – sorry – Beluga for Adam, a piñata of miaow miaow and pick and mix imported from Mexico please. Also Calvin Harris, Riverdance, some jam in little plastic containers . . .

Swill You know the free ones you get.

Agent Squirty cream – or clotted if you've got it, Cliff Richard and his orchestra, a Miami club . . .

Mary Mirror balls.

Agent   Yep – did you get that? Sorry caviar and maybe some blinis (or crackers if not). (*Improvisation with audience asking for requests.*) That's everything I think. Thanks so much. Says the taxi won't be long.

Mary (*on mic*)   Shame we're not all here isn't it, Adam? How was Eve last time you saw her? When you last *popped* in?

She stops music.

Agent   She was good actually, Adam, she sent love – didn't I tell you? I decided to surprise her! There was this tree and she was . . . (*Mimes beautiful tree and* **Eve**.) Like this. (*Bends over, proffers arse.*) Stank like shit. Didn't see me at first. Hi Eve – Evie pie – only me. Hey that's no way to greet an old friend.

Mimes **Eve** *not noticing him, then spotting him, scared.* **Agent** *forces kisses on cheeks then mouth.*

Agent   'Come' . . . I close my eyes when I kiss. Bit of an old romantic. 'Eve – sssh. Come on.'

Mimes game of chase round tree trunk.

Mimes grabbing her wrist round the tree trunk; moves round to wrap arm around her shoulders. Knees her between the legs. Switch to **Eve**'s *reaction, almost buckled.*

Agent   'Please Please.'

Then mimes hand grabbing her hair and pulling her backwards by it. Switch to **Agent**, *hand holding her hair, pulling her over backwards and grabbing her neck to turn her round.*

Agent   So I just. (*Lifts her skirt. Switches to* **Eve**, *bent against wall, and flicks up skirt behind him.*) Really easy actually, easier than you think. (*Switches back to* **Agent** *behind her, pulls down her pants/tights, opens his own flies, and begins mime rape.*) 'I'm a nice man, Eve. You know – people like me. I went to university. I was in the choir.' (*Withdraws from* **Eve**. *Pauses to look at* **Adam**. *Pulls mimed penknife from pocket, opens blade.*) That enough . . . Adam . . .?

Adam *stands and looks at audience.*

Eve *enters out of the final cherry delivery. An avenging fury – she's lit with ice-cold rage.* **Agent** *holds position for a moment – it's clear she has seen.* **Eve** *with audience.*

Eve   Good evening. Very good evening. An excellent evening. Don't get up. You just sit there in your seats. (*To* **Agent**.) I would fashion you into a lovely toilette – open your mouth it's not open wide enough so I'd cut it with a scalpel – place myself upon you and not a seed left of humanity – not a seed – not a seed left. And I'd open you up – place myself upon you – talk to you as I evacuated and I would say let's go through the rules. First of all – don't touch me that way – no no no – down you go.

(*To* **Swill**.) Is it funny – why is that funny? IT'S NOT FUNNY. 'COME ON PEOPLE!' . . . 'WHO DOESN'T LOVE FREEDOM?' Freedom from what exactly? Mary's mouthpiece – her little bitch – slippery as a butcher's dick. (*Spits.*) Hello, Mary . . . you should say 'Hello Eve'.

Mary   You should have RSVP'd really – etiquette, etc.

Eve (*speed builds, words tumbling out*)   Funny seeing the old place again. Such majesty – what heights we've reached! I've come back for the ending. The final moments before darkness falls! Oh I adored you, Mary – hobbling about behind you on my one glittering heel – 'Lucky me' I crowed – 'god's chosen disciple'. Cos oh it's bliss up here isn't it? Away from the filth. And hey – HEY – what's wrong with that?

Mary   Nothing as it happens. HQ gave us the all clear, oh . . . didn't you know?

Eve   CONGRATULATIONS, MARY, BUT I'M TALKING NOW. Ever since I stuffed your forbidden fruit in my greedy chops in the dead of night, I've been scratching. Strange fruit. Sour and strange – bitter. I scratched and scratched. Not cherries, Mary – blood – and you're drenched in it.

Drunk on it. YOUR little EVE – the bitch with scabies –
scratched beneath your little paradise til her fingers bled.

Mary   It's just the way the world works, Eve, what can you
do eh, Adam? What can you do eh?

Eve   Adam. You didn't come, Adam. What are you, Adam?
Adam. Are you this? Are you that? That's it – stand there
nice and quiet. Oh they keep it quiet. (*To audience.*) You're
quiet too.

Mary (*half an eye on the audience*)   The civilised they will eat
each other, Eve.

Eve   DAMN YOUR SMILING. WHERE'S IT ALL GONE,
MARY? WHERE'S IT ALL GONE? HUMANITY?
JUSTICE? LOVE? LOST. YOU'VE NICKED 'EM.
HAVEN'T YOU FUCKFACE? THIS IS FOR THE LITTLE
PEOPLE, MARY, THE LITTLE PEOPLE. LIKE ME. DO
WE STINK, MARY? SO SORRY. DO WE REEK? SO
SORRY. IF IT'S A PROBLEM I'M GONNA SHIT RIGHT
HERE AND YOU'RE GONNA SMELL IT YOU'RE
GONNA FEEL THE FILTH. (*Spits.*) WE'RE NOT ASKING
FOR YOUR PITY – MARY. DON'T YOU PITY EVE. C
MINUS EVE, STUPID EVE, EVE OF THE SHITTY
MASSES, WRETCHED EVE. DON'T YOU PITY EVE FOR
I AM FIRE AND I WILL BURN HELLFIRE. WE'RE
HAVING BACK WHAT YOU OWE, MARY: THE RICHES
YOU'VE ROBBED – THE LIVES YOU'VE SUCKED DRY
– IN HER WAS FOUND ALL THE WEALTH OF ALL THE
EARTH – OH 'MARY MARY' HAVEN'S COMING DOWN
TO EARTH AND YOU'RE GONNA PAY UP. WE ARE
WITHOUT MERCY AMEN. (*As she pours cherry blood into
onstage bucket.*) Goodbye, cherry pie.

Drowns **Mary** *in a yellow bucket in the pit.*

Looks and looks. Long pause.

Eve   Not a word? What, nothing? Why don't you cry out?

This is how it must be. To end this long night of our captivity, this degradation, and take back the riches of justice and freedom. It is our work. It is yours and yours and yours and yours. *People* will do this. And I swear it has already begun.

Eve *and* **Mary** *remain in scene in the pit. Rest of gang speak in hushed tones from the edges of the space into mics, they are close to the audience as darkness slowly falls.*

Agent   Gosh . . . I feel better. That was – what's the word?

Swill   Cathartic. I agree, I feel purged.

Adam   I'm looking forward to the new world – the fairer world.

Swill   I feel empowered – public outcry, the headlines forced governments to act.

Agent   No one's above the law anymore – not multinationals, not celebrities, not politicians. I feel confident.

Adam   The revolution's here. It'll take time but there's no going back.

Swill   Humanity's pulled it out of the bag.

Agent   I've never felt so optimistic. Thank you, Eve.

Eve   No problem.

Blackout. Long pause. Final music starts in the darkness. Spotlight fades up on **Mary***'s body, head in bucket. She laughs, picks herself up, the gang's eyes sparkle, they grin. UV lights pick out 'Deus Ex Machina' graffitti'd across the walls.*

Mary   How could you ever think I'd go
       However hard you try
       Stab me through my open palms
       I bleed but never die

Gang place huge, filthy wings on **Mary***.*

And they've tried so many times before
People never learn
We're flying for the sun, flying for the sun
Together
And together we will burn

Huge production kicks in, fans, glitter falls, mirror balls turn.

Cos I'm stronger
Stronger than you will ever see
You're so good for me
I'm growing now
A kingdom like the rise
Of the surging sea
It all belongs to me
And if you think you're alone, my love
Open up your chest and
You'll find my name
Is printed on your heart
Cos you know
I told you
I tried to tell you
I really tried to tell you
Did you forget
I'm a god?
Never forget
I'm a god
And so that's amen . . .
I'm a god.

Blackout.

DRAMA ONLINE

A new way to study drama

From curriculum classics
to contemporary writing
Accompanied by
theory and practice

Discover. Read. Study. Perform.

Find out more:
www.dramaonlinelibrary.com

BLOOMSBURY

methuen
drama

THE ARDEN
SHAKESPEARE

FABER
DIGITAL

Bloomsbury Methuen Drama Modern Plays

include work by

Bola Agbaje
Edward Albee
Davey Anderson
Jean Anouilh
John Arden
Peter Barnes
Sebastian Barry
Alistair Beaton
Brendan Behan
Edward Bond
William Boyd
Bertolt Brecht
Howard Brenton
Amelia Bullmore
Anthony Burgess
Leo Butler
Jim Cartwright
Lolita Chakrabarti
Caryl Churchill
Lucinda Coxon
Curious Directive
Nick Darke
Shelagh Delaney
Ishy Din
Claire Dowie
David Edgar
David Eldridge
Dario Fo
Michael Frayn
John Godber
Paul Godfrey
James Graham
David Greig
John Guare
Mark Haddon
Peter Handke
David Harrower
Jonathan Harvey
Iain Heggie

Robert Holman
Caroline Horton
Terry Johnson
Sarah Kane
Barrie Keeffe
Doug Lucie
Anders Lustgarten
David Mamet
Patrick Marber
Martin McDonagh
Arthur Miller
D. C. Moore
Tom Murphy
Phyllis Nagy
Anthony Neilson
Peter Nichols
Joe Orton
Joe Penhall
Luigi Pirandello
Stephen Poliakoff
Lucy Prebble
Peter Quilter
Mark Ravenhill
Philip Ridley
Willy Russell
Jean-Paul Sartre
Sam Shepard
Martin Sherman
Wole Soyinka
Simon Stephens
Peter Straughan
Kate Tempest
Theatre Workshop
Judy Upton
Timberlake Wertenbaker
Roy Williams
Snoo Wilson
Frances Ya-Chu Cowhig
Benjamin Zephaniah

Bloomsbury Methuen Drama Contemporary Dramatists

include

John Arden (two volumes)
Arden & D'Arcy
Peter Barnes (three volumes)
Sebastian Barry
Mike Bartlett
Dermot Bolger
Edward Bond (eight volumes)
Howard Brenton (two volumes)
Leo Butler
Richard Cameron
Jim Cartwright
Caryl Churchill (two volumes)
Complicite
Sarah Daniels (two volumes)
Nick Darke
David Edgar (three volumes)
David Eldridge (two volumes)
Ben Elton
Per Olov Enquist
Dario Fo (two volumes)
Michael Frayn (four volumes)
John Godber (four volumes)
Paul Godfrey
James Graham
David Greig
John Guare
Lee Hall (two volumes)
Katori Hall
Peter Handke
Jonathan Harvey (two volumes)
Iain Heggie
Israel Horovitz
Declan Hughes
Terry Johnson (three volumes)
Sarah Kane
Barrie Keeffe
Bernard-Marie Koltès (two volumes)
Franz Xaver Kroetz
Kwame Kwei-Armah
David Lan
Bryony Lavery
Deborah Levy
Doug Lucie

David Mamet (four volumes)
Patrick Marber
Martin McDonagh
Duncan McLean
David Mercer (two volumes)
Anthony Minghella (two volumes)
Tom Murphy (six volumes)
Phyllis Nagy
Anthony Neilson (two volumes)
Peter Nichol (two volumes)
Philip Osment
Gary Owen
Louise Page
Stewart Parker (two volumes)
Joe Penhall (two volumes)
Stephen Poliakoff (three volumes)
David Rabe (two volumes)
Mark Ravenhill (three volumes)
Christina Reid
Philip Ridley (two volumes)
Willy Russell
Eric-Emmanuel Schmitt
Ntozake Shange
Sam Shepard (two volumes)
Martin Sherman (two volumes)
Christopher Shinn
Joshua Sobel
Wole Soyinka (two volumes)
Simon Stephens (three volumes)
Shelagh Stephenson
David Storey (three volumes)
C. P. Taylor
Sue Townsend
Judy Upton
Michel Vinaver (two volumes)
Arnold Wesker (two volumes)
Peter Whelan
Michael Wilcox
Roy Williams (four volumes)
David Williamson
Snoo Wilson (two volumes)
David Wood (two volumes)
Victoria Wood

Bloomsbury Methuen Drama Student Editions

Jean Anouilh *Antigone* • John Arden *Serjeant Musgrave's Dance* • Alan Ayckbourn *Confusions* • Aphra Behn *The Rover* • Edward Bond *Lear* • *Saved* • Bertolt Brecht *The Caucasian Chalk Circle* • *Fear and Misery in the Third Reich* • *The Good Person of Szechwan* • *Life of Galileo* • *Mother Courage and Her Children* • *The Resistible Rise of Arturo Ui* • *The Threepenny Opera* • Anton Chekhov *The Cherry Orchard* • *The Seagull* • *Three Sisters* • *Uncle Vanya* • Caryl Churchill *Serious Money* • *Top Girls* • Shelagh Delaney *A Taste of Honey* • Euripides *Elektra* • *Medea* • Dario Fo *Accidental Death of an Anarchist* • Michael Frayn *Copenhagen* • John Galsworthy *Strife* • Nikolai Gogol *The Government Inspector* • Carlo Goldoni *A Servant to Two Masters* • Lorraine Hansberry *A Raisin in the Sun* • Robert Holman *Across Oka* • Henrik Ibsen *A Doll's House* • *Ghosts* • *Hedda Gabler* • Sarah Kane *4.48 Psychosis* • *Blasted* • Charlotte Keatley *My Mother Said I Never Should* • Bernard Kops *Dreams of Anne Frank* • Federico García Lorca *Blood Wedding* • *Doña Rosita the Spinster* (bilingual edition) • *The House of Bernarda Alba* (bilingual edition) • *Yerma* (bilingual edition) • David Mamet *Glengarry Glen Ross* • *Oleanna* • Patrick Marber *Closer* • John Marston *The Malcontent* • Martin McDonagh *The Lieutenant of Inishmore* • *The Lonesome West* • *The Beauty Queen of Leenane* • Arthur Miller *All My Sons* • *The Crucible* • *A View from the Bridge* • *Death of a Salesman* • *The Price* • *After the Fall* • *The Last Yankee* • *A Memory of Two Mondays* • *Broken Glass* • Joe Orton *Loot* • Joe Penhall *Blue/Orange* • Luigi Pirandello *Six Characters in Search of an Author* • Lucy Prebble *Enron* • Mark Ravenhill *Shopping and F***ing* • Willy Russell *Blood Brothers* • *Educating Rita* • Sophocles *Antigone* • *Oedipus the King* • Wole Soyinka *Death and the King's Horseman* • Shelagh Stephenson *The Memory of Water* • August Strindberg *Miss Julie* • J. M. Synge *The Playboy of the Western World* • Theatre Workshop *Oh What a Lovely War* • Frank Wedekind *Spring Awakening* • Timberlake Wertenbaker *Our Country's Good* • Arnold Wesker *The Merchant* • Oscar Wilde *The Importance of Being Earnest* • Tennessee Williams *A Streetcar Named Desire* • *The Glass Menagerie* • *Cat on a Hot Tin Roof* • *Sweet Bird of Youth*

For a complete listing of Bloomsbury
Methuen Drama titles, visit:
www.bloomsbury.com/drama

Follow us on Twitter and keep up to date
with our news and publications
@MethuenDrama